Nehemiah

I AM—TAKING AUTHORITY OVER IDENTITY

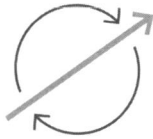

MIKE HILSON

D0873153

wesleyan
PUBLISHING HOUSE
wphstore.com
Indianapolis, Indiana

Copyright © 2020 by Mike Hilson
Published by Wesleyan Publishing House
Indianapolis, Indiana 46250
Printed in the United States of America
ISBN: 978-1-63257-340-7
ISBN (e-book): 978-1-63257-341-4

Library of Congress Control Number: 2019952793

Contents

Acknowledgments

Thank you to my wife, Tina, who has been my partner in life and ministry. I love you!

To our three boys, Robert, Stephen, and Joshua, thank you for taking this journey of ministry with us and having a great attitude about it along the way.

Thank you also to my spiritual family at New Life Church for giving me the freedom to grow as a leader and follower of Christ.

Most importantly, I want to thank and praise God!

About This Book

People sometimes ask why I would take the time to write a book. The answer is twofold. First, it's an opportunity to speak with my children, grandchildren, and great-grandchildren about this wonderful gospel that I've had the honor of working for all my life. I want them to see the joy and power of living a life guided and protected by God's Word, God's Spirit, and God's commands. In doing so, I hope to establish many generations of my family in the wonderful grace of our Lord. So I write as a father.

I also write as a pastor. New Life Church has become a rather large body of believers meeting in multiple services and multiple locations across multiple states. While this is a huge reason to praise God—and more of a blessing than any of us who work here could ever have hoped for—it creates its own set of challenges. It has become impossible for me to sit down individually with folks in the church, like I once did, to have deeper conversations about the power of God's Word and how it can be applied in their lives. This is the reason I decided to write a series of books called *Coffee with the Pastor*.

While I am neither a theologian nor a scholar, as a pastor, my job is to help people read and better understand the Word of God. His Word is powerful and life changing. If you read and understand it, you can see the God of heaven through the blood of Jesus and the power of the Holy Spirit—and that will change your life. Therefore, the goal of this series of books is not theological, but a practical application of life-changing, biblical truth. That is the purpose of my ministry and the ultimate goal of my life.

So, grab a cup of coffee, open up your Bible, and let's get you thinking about what God can do in your life.

Introduction

The life of Nehemiah, as recorded in the Bible, has been a great source of insight and encouragement for me for many years. When, as a young pastor, I first studied Nehemiah's story, his persistence and wisdom in the face of opposition and difficulty inspired me. That inspiration has returned many times throughout my career and my life.

Nehemiah's life is a clear example of God's providential power to have the right person in the right place at the right time. With Jerusalem under Syrian control, Nehemiah found himself at the side of the only man in the world who could give authority and provide resources to restore the city of God: King Artaxerxes. Nehemiah's journey from slave to rebuilder of a city, and ultimately to rebuilder of a nation is one of the great leadership stories in all of Scripture.

As we study the biblical book that bears Nehemiah's name, we find hope for all that God has planned for us. Nehemiah was certainly not the most obvious candidate to play the hero in the story of the rebuilding of Jerusalem. As a slave in the king's service, he was severely limited in his ability to secure the change and leadership that was needed for his beloved homeland. As one who had lived his entire life in Syria, he was considered a foreigner by those who had remained in the homeland—those he would be called to lead. But God is not limited by our own self-image or by what others see as our potential. In this account, we will see that no matter how restricted your self-identity, God has the power to take you far beyond those restrictions. You just need to trust him. He has an identity set up for you, and his definition of you is the best definition. Though you may have a self-identity—or what I like to call an *I-am*—that is established through a lifetime of mistakes, miscues, and failures, God still sees all that he made you to be. And if you let him, he can make you all of that and more!

As we look at the life of Nehemiah, we will do so through the lens of six different identities that Nehemiah experienced in his life and work. By looking into these identities, both positive and negative, we can discover how he overcame the negative and destructive identities and worked effectively through the positive and constructive ones. We will also find clues to our own feelings of failure and inadequacy that will help us to move from a damaged, destructive I-am to a God-inspired I-am. Along the way, we will deal with our own short-sightedness and lack of faith when it comes to our personal identity.

Keep in mind as you read this that we are reading from the Old Testament. The Old Testament of our Bible is the covenant of God with the people of Israel and how that agreement played out between them throughout their history. Therefore, the Old Testament is best read as narrative in nature. While we often cannot draw direct instruction from the Old Testament, we can learn how our God leads, how our God views and works with us, and how we should follow.

So, let's get started.

PART 1

THE POWER OF I-AM

Your "I-am" will determine your "I will" every time.

Most people's level of achievement is consistent with their personal definition and understanding of their own self-worth, ability, and identity. While occasional outliers may achieve beyond these self-imposed limitations, most will never even attempt to strive for anything perceived to be outside the boundaries of their own self-definition. These limitations are based on a person's I-am—their sense of identity. A person's I-am sets the direction and path of that individual's future and potential.

The problem is not in the *existence* of a person's I-am, but in the *source* of their I-am. Most people allow their circle of friends or their culture to define their I-am.

As a pastor, I seek to challenge our culture's practice of labeling individuals and groups with broad, sweeping generalizations. Such labels are often unhelpful and even downright unhealthy. By labeling others, our society limits people's God-given, God-ordained potential, instead allowing a set of shallow, surface characteristics to define a person's entire life. In most cases, our friends and family, even our culture, are trying to be helpful by sorting people into categories. They may think, "If she can just accept who she is, life will be easier, and she will be able to find peace." Unfortunately, those labels and categories are often allowed to solidify to the point that they become an entrapment. Much like having one's feet hardened into concrete, these hardened identities hold us back, slow us down, and, depending on the circumstances, can even drown us. Once this hardened I-am is firmly set, it is believed by culture and by most individuals to be permanent and irrevocable.

Many of us are trapped inside of our own I-am.

This can lead to anger, depression, and dangerous behavior, as individuals who are unhappy with their declared and hardened identity begin to blame themselves, family, friends, culture, or even God for the mess that they have become. Individuals are trapped in a victimhood that cannot be overcome. Once this I-am is firmly set, even those who love us will insist that we need to just accept it for what it is and move on with life in our "new normal."

One example of this problem is clearly spelled out by Warren Farrell in his book *The Boy Crisis*:

Historically, a boy's journey to prove himself is what gave him that sense of purpose. Most cultures, to survive, assigned each sex Mars/Venus-type roles that were "sold" to each sex as its purpose in life. These underlying goals of both parents' roles-as-purpose were to optimize their children's chance of survival and make their children's lives better than theirs.

But . . . as developed countries had the luxury to permit divorce, they responded by creating the "era of the multi-option woman" (raise children, raise money, or some combination of both) while continuing the historic "era of the no-option man." That is, a dad's "three options" were still raise money, raise money, or raise money. However, with women often sharing the breadwinner role, a young man could no longer find his purpose as a man by being a sole breadwinner. And, as fewer warriors were needed, boys began experiencing a "purpose void."[1]

In his book, Farrell points out that this "purpose void leads to increasing levels of suicide, crime, mass shootings, depression, and unemployment."[2] The hardened concrete of male identity markers that no longer work is causing many males to simply drown in the waters of societal and personal expectations.

There seems to be no hope. But that is not how God sees the situation!

The apostle Paul writes to the church in Corinth, "Therefore, if anyone is in Christ, the new creation has come: The old has gone, the new is here!" (2 Cor. 5:17). There is hope for a new I-am in Christ Jesus. This is a truth that our culture desperately needs to learn and understand. This truth can bring hope and freedom to so many. While we may live in a culture that questions its need for forgiveness from sin—and even questions the existence of anything called *sin* at all—it is also a culture that is desperate for personal, internal, and even miraculous change! Our culture seems to be open to spiritual pathways to internal change in greater ways than I have seen in my lifetime. Culture may well be hesitant to trust the church or any institutional religion, but people are hungry for a spiritual experience that gives hope and power to their lives.

This book is about that hope.

The I-Am Cycle

Each of us is caught in a cycle.

This cycle may be positive or negative, constructive or destructive, or it may simply be a static cycle of repetition with no real progress forward. Whatever the effect this cycle is having in our lives, it is real. For some, this cycle is healthy. For others, not so much.

The Strong I-Am

Many people have a strong sense of I-am and have applied specific strategies of self-discipline to increase the strength of their identity. These folks even see it as possible to expand their I-am to include areas of success unseen by others in their fields or communities. These people simply need to reinforce the God-given truth of their potential and focus their efforts to become everything God has made them to be. If this is you, stay with it! The Bible has a word for you on this: "Let us not become weary in doing good, for at the proper time we will reap a harvest if we do not give up" (Gal. 6:9). Your efforts, centered in God's will, Jesus' cleansing, and the Holy Spirit's empowerment, will bring you to a wonderful realization of all that God has for you. His love for you will carry you to ever-increasing heights of success and ever-widening depths of understanding.

The Weak I-Am

Many people do not have such a strong sense of I-am. Though they are living a good life and are striving to be good people, there is no sense of overcoming or victory in life. Life, to these people, seems to be a series of struggles with limited success. They may be good people, kind people, and people who help people, yet they just cannot seem to get ahead. This group needs insight into how to increase the level of success in life. Together, we will discover pathways to success in following God, helping others, and improving your I-am.

This success will not be based solely on your own strength. There is a greater strength available to you that can help you overcome in areas that have traditionally not been success stories for you. This power is from God, the Holy Spirit. This is simply God's presence living and working inside of you to give you strength you did not originally have.

In times of desperation or senseless failure, we may feel that there is no way to succeed. But God sees our frustration and hurt, and desires to help us in those moments. Even when we cannot figure out what the problem really is, the Holy Spirit understands. In his letter to the Christians in Rome, the apostle Paul wrote, "In the same way, the Spirit helps us in our weakness. We do not know what we ought to pray for, but the Spirit himself intercedes for us through wordless groans. And he who searches our hearts knows the mind of the Spirit, because the Spirit intercedes for God's people in accordance with the will of God" (Rom. 8:26–27).

There is strength for you!

The Destructive I-Am

Some have an I-am that is destructive. These types of identities can play out in many different ways. They range from the narcissist who truly believes that no one else matters but him or herself, to the angry parent who abuses their spouse and children, to the frustrated addict who cannot accept that he or she is trapped in anything that affects anyone else, to the depressed, who can see no path forward and wonders whether the world would be better without them.

Let's be clear: all of these are lies!

The apostle Peter wrote a letter in which he warned, "Your enemy the devil prowls around like a roaring lion looking for someone to devour" (1 Pet. 5:8). Our enemy does not prowl about like we see in so many movies. He is not hiding around corners ready to pounce on us when we walk by, nor is he skulking around with some pitchfork and pointy tail trying to jump inside of us and turn us into the antichrist. No, his methods are the same as they have always been. If he can confuse our own sense of I-am and who God is, then he leaves us in a painful, confusing world without the support and help of a loving God. This can drive some people to a pattern of living that is destructive to themselves or those around them.

It is our position in creation—"God created mankind in his own image" (Gen. 1:27)—that sets us apart from the animal kingdom. While wild animals naturally kill each other for food, mates, territory, or protection, we are made a little above that. We have the capacity for all of that violence and death, but we also have the capacity to understand that no one individual is more important than all the others. We have the capacity to look at others and see more than food or competition. We have the capacity to look at the weak and wounded and see more than just an easy meal or a weak competitor. Because we are made in the image of God, we can be compassionate, caring, and even self-depriving, when it is helpful to others. With only a few exceptions, wild animals don't do that. But if the enemy of our soul can convince us that God is not there—or even that God is not good—he may be able to cause us to act like animals toward one another. This I-am pattern is the most frightening, and yet still, God offers hope and freedom. In his letter to the church in Rome, the apostle Paul wrote, "Who will rescue me from this body that is subject to death? Thanks be to God, who delivers me through Jesus Christ our Lord!" (Rom. 7:24–25).

If your version of I-am is playing out in destructive ways, please keep reading and find the hope and freedom God has for you. However, I also strongly encourage you to find someone to talk to. A counselor or a pastor can help you think all of this through, and find positive and constructive ways to reverse the destructive trends in your life. Be strong enough to admit your need for help, and go find it. Honestly, if you cannot find other heroes in your life and cannot yet accept the truth that God can be the hero you need, then choose to be your own hero and find someone who can help you change patterns that are not serving you well.

The three I-am categories described above are not a complete list of human states of mind. We are incredibly complex creatures with immense capacity for both good and evil. This journey will be all about establishing the identity that will determine which pathway we ultimately choose to take.

Identity Establishes Truth

This I-am problem is not new.

From the very beginning of time our identity has been threatened. In the biblical account of Adam and Eve in the garden of Eden, we see a loving couple living in true utopian peace. That peace was shattered, not by war, natural disaster, or disease, but by a loss of proper identity. God had placed the couple "in the Garden of Eden to work it and take care of it" (Gen. 2:15). In this perfect setting, God established only one rule, "You must not eat from the tree of the knowledge of good and evil, for when you eat from it you will certainly die" (v. 17). The identities were simple and clear-cut: God was the authority figure and Adam and Eve were the caretakers. They were free to use anything in the garden, with the exception of the one tree.

Not complicated—at least, not until someone changed the identity roles.

"Now the serpent was more crafty than any of the wild animals the LORD God had made" (Gen. 3:1). This serpent, who represents the enemy of our souls, Satan, was "crafty" enough to know that he could not get this first couple to leave God and serve him outright. But what if he could get them to question God's I-am as ruler and their I-am as caretakers? What if he could get them to reject their God-given identity and receive one that he chose for them? So, he posed a simple question, "Did God really say . . . ?" (v. 1), followed by a challenge to their given reality, "You will not certainly die" (v. 4), and then landed the knockout blow with an appeal to the pride he knew was dormant inside of each of them: "God knows that when you eat from it your eyes will be opened, and you will be like God" (v. 5). By changing the identities within the garden, he was successful in destroying the peace and balance of the garden.

Now, regardless of how you view that account of creation, there is a truth to be learned here. Proper understanding of identity brings stability and peace, while improper assignment of identity can bring discord and pain. When you attempt to live out an I-am that is not true for you, it is disruptive to your health and balance. An improper I-am will cause you to think in wrong ways. The serpent knew that the death from eating the fruit was not going to be literal, instant, physical death, but rather a separation from the life that had been so peaceful and fulfilling up to that point. And so, by simply altering the truth slightly, he destroyed the balance entirely. By changing the way these two identified themselves, he changed the way they thought about themselves and their surroundings. He changed their truth.

Where once God was their protector, now he was their barrier. Satan convinced them that God had misled them, and so they ate.

Where once the garden was home, now it seemed like a limitation. They wanted to be like God and see the world beyond this garden, so they had their eyes opened.

Where once God was their friend, he now seemed like a threat, so they hid.

When their personal identity changed, it shifted their personal truth. This new truth would prove to be their undoing.

Your identity establishes your truth, and once these have changed, you start thinking differently.

Which brings us to the second point in this process.

Truth Establishes Thinking

In the previous section, we said that identity establishes truth. This leads to what I call the "I am therefore I think" problem.

Your I-am—the truth you allow to take hold about your identity—will establish the way you see and think about the world around you. In the case of Adam and Eve, their I-am, as set by God, was to be caretakers of the garden. Within that identity they were able to function in the peace, tranquility, and balance of the garden. When they later embraced an I-am that was not given to them by God but rather sold to them by the serpent, they lost the innocence of their original I-am perspective: "Then the eyes of both of them were opened, and they realized they were naked" (Gen. 3:7). They lost confidence: "Then the man and his wife heard the sound of the LORD God as he was walking in the garden in the cool of the day, and they hid" (v. 8). And, ultimately, they lost their home: "So the LORD God banished him from the Garden of Eden" (v. 23).

In short, they lost everything!

When our identity changes our truth, our thinking changes along with it. We process our surroundings out of the truth established by our identity. There is an old adage that says, "When you are a hammer, everything looks like a nail." There is great truth in this saying. We tend to see everything through the lens of our own personal truth, and this affects how we think. To the salesman, everyone is a potential customer. To the entertainer, everyone is a potential audience member. To the politician, everyone is a potential voter. To the pastor, everyone is a potential convert. Our understanding of our identity is crucial, because it sets the lens through which we think about our surroundings.

Once our thinking has shifted, our actions change with it.

Thinking Establishes Action

The way we think affects the way we act, which leads to the "I am, therefore I think, so I will" problem.

Our accepted and established identity, our I-am, sets the truth about ourselves. This truth, set by our identity, establishes our thinking about the world around us, and that thinking eventually results in action. We act out based on how we think about the world around us.

When Adam and Eve allowed their identity to shift—from the one given to them by God to the one sold to them by the serpent—they shifted from being caretakers to wanna-be gods. The serpent told them, "God knows that when you eat from it [the fruit of the forbidden tree] your eyes will be opened, and you will be like God, knowing good and evil" (Gen. 3:5). While they were perfectly capable of fulfilling their identity of caretaker, they were woefully and entirely inadequate to the role of being god. Once they knew more of what God knew, they did not find it empowering or freeing. Instead, they became filled with shame and fear. Where once they were "both naked, and they felt no shame" (Gen. 2:25), they now "sewed fig leaves together and made coverings for themselves" (Gen. 3:7). Where once they took walks with God in the cool of the day, now "they hid from the Lord God" (v. 8). Unfortunately, the steep price of living outside of their God-given identity didn't end there. A little-noticed verse reveals that, for the first time, death entered creation as a recorded part of humanity's story: "The Lord God made garments of skin for Adam and his wife and clothed them" (v. 21). In the New Testament, the apostle Paul said that "the wages of sin is death" (Rom. 6:23). This truth played out in vivid reality in the garden, costing some poor animal its life and shifting the thinking and actions of Adam and Eve forever.

Unfortunately this faulty thinking did not stop there. The offspring of Adam and Eve, all of humanity, has continued to live in fear and shame and in pursuit of becoming our own gods. What started as an identity shift that caused a truth change, a new way of thinking and acting, became a habitual pattern of rebellion against God.

Action Establishes Habit

My accepted "I-am" will ultimately set the course of actions that I take, which leads us into the "I-am, therefore I think, therefore I will, therefore I do" problem.

Rejection of our God-given I-am can permanently change our truth, thinking, and actions. Sometimes those changes are not ones that we would choose, but rather consequences that we are stuck with. God told the serpent, "You will crawl on your belly and you will eat dust all the days of your life" (Gen. 3:14). He told Eve, "I will make your pains in childbearing very severe" (v. 16). And to Adam he said, "Cursed is the ground because of you; through painful toil you will eat from it all the days of your life" (v. 17). These consequences would become our "new normal" and be established as habits that we simply receive as inevitable. As we work through the consequences of our chosen identity, we inevitably establish new habits that further harden the concrete of our accepted I-am, even if it is not what seems right or best to us. Like Adam and Eve, we settle into what seems like a broken and cursed existence, and our habits drive our identity further into the setting concrete of our consciousness.

Unless there is a miraculous way out, we are forever stuck.

But what if there were a way out? What if somehow our I-am could be reset?

God Resets Identity

Now we come to the "I am God's" solution.

The apostle Paul, in his letter to the Christians in Rome, established Christian understanding about what Jesus did for us through his life, death, and resurrection. By the time Jesus arrived on the scene, it had been accepted for millennia that the sin of Adam set the I-am of all mankind. Paul put it this way: "Therefore, just as sin entered the world through one man, and death through sin, and in this way death came to all people, because all sinned" (Rom. 5:12). Humanity desperately needed a remedy for sin, or disobeying God's commands. Just like Adam and Eve, each of us has faced moments in our lives when we knew what God would have us do—or not do—and we have chosen against God. The people of God have called that *sin* since the garden of Eden. And that habitual pattern of sin set in each of us by Adam himself continually hardens the "I am a sinner" identity that haunts and stalks all of us. That particular I-am sets our truth, thinking, actions, and habits. Once we personally find ourselves habitually choosing against God, we begin to harden the concrete around our own feet and find ourselves trapped in the age-old identity of sinner.

But Paul continues. "But the gift is not like the trespass. For if the many died by the trespass of the one man, how much more did God's grace and the gift that came by the grace of the one man, Jesus Christ, overflow to the many! Nor can the gift of God be compared with the result of the one man's sin: The judgment followed one sin and brought condemnation, but the gift followed many trespasses and brought justification" (Rom. 5:15–16).

So Jesus, by his death on the cross, paid the price for our sin, and by his resurrection from the dead, he set us free from our bondage. In other words, Jesus reset our I-am.

Before Jesus, "I am a sinner." After Jesus, "I am redeemed, remade, reset, and renewed."

Our I-am has been reset by our Savior, Jesus Christ!

The Journey to a Healthy I-Am

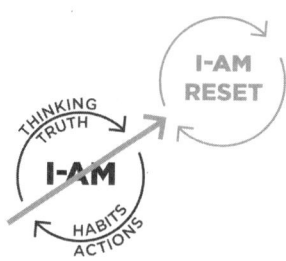

It is in the context of this reality that we will look into the rest of our journey together. While the story we will take up here is in the Old Testament, we must understand it from the lens of the New Testament. The requirements and specifics of following God and being righteous that we will read in Nehemiah's account are based on a contract or covenant that God made with Israel around 3,500 years ago. We must understand Nehemiah's story through that lens. But application of that story must be made through the lens of a new contract or covenant that Jesus made with all humanity. Through his sacrifice and resurrection, we have a better deal than the

Old Testament folks had. However, we must look at all of this with the realization that God's goal with humanity is always to forgive and to reestablish the relationship that was broken all the way back in the garden of Eden. This entire story is important for us to understand if we are to fully realize the depth and height of God's miraculous deliverance in our lives. While the truths we find in the life of Nehemiah may play out in an old covenant reality, the truths of the heart of God and his ability to reset our I-am remain the same, if not stronger than they were in Nehemiah's day. We can find our way out of the trap that old serpent has bound us into, and we can do it through the power, love, and grace of Jesus our Redeemer!

You don't have to remain stuck in that old I-am. You can be reset, remade, renewed, and redeemed!

Now, let Nehemiah give you some pointers on following the God of your real I-am!

PART 2

I AM BROKEN

The words of Nehemiah son of Hakaliah: In the month of Kislev in the twentieth year, while I was in the citadel of Susa, Hanani, one of my brothers, came from Judah with some other men, and I questioned them about the Jewish remnant that had survived the exile, and also about Jerusalem. They said to me, "Those who survived the exile and are back in the province are in great trouble and disgrace. The wall of Jerusalem is broken down, and its gates have been burned with fire." When I heard these things, I sat down and wept. For some days I mourned and fasted and prayed before the God of heaven.

—Nehemiah 1:1–4

About 150 years had passed since King Nebuchadnezzar destroyed Jerusalem and took many of the brightest young Hebrews as captives to Babylon. Until the arrival of Ezra and later Nehemiah to rebuild the city, what remained of the capital city of the Israelites from this destruction was a burned out, defenseless shell filled with a constantly besieged population. Those who lived there were unprotected by any army and unguarded by any walls. As a result of this lack of protection, the people living there were constantly being invaded by neighboring tribes and peoples. As they worked to grow produce, raise livestock, and save up resources, these other tribes and peoples would simply attack the unprotected city and steal all that they had worked to gather. The situation was truly dire, and life inside the city without walls must have been incredibly difficult.

But Nehemiah was in Susa. He was in the capital city of the most powerful nation in the known world at the time. He was a direct servant to King Artaxerxes and was living a very comfortable life. He was unaware of the true situation on the ground in Jerusalem, a city he had heritage in, but had likely never visited. He wondered about this city that he had probably heard stories about for his entire life.

At the first opportunity, Nehemiah jumped at the chance to get an eyewitness report from Jerusalem. The news was not good. He was devastated by what he heard. Citizens of the United States would be devastated by any attack on or damage to its capital city, Washington, DC. This emotion would bring us closer to understanding Nehemiah's emotional state in light of this news, but even this would fall short. Washington, DC, is the nation's capital and holds many of its treasures and iconic memorials and museums, but to the Jewish people,

Jerusalem was more than that. Jerusalem represented not only the political and governmental center of Jewish life; it also represented the spiritual center of Jewish life. Jerusalem lying in ruins was tantamount to the very Jewish identity lying in ruins. Nehemiah was crushed by the thought of such disgrace being heaped on his people, his nation, his city, his home.

In the course of our lives we will all face crushing moments in which the all-encompassing sorrow of devastating loss can lead to depression. Ultimately, they can lead to forming an I-am that identifies us as broken. However, accepting brokenness as our identity can have life-threatening results. In this section, we'll look at how Nehemiah handled his overwhelming sadness and brokenness. Along the way, we'll find God-inspired ways to overcome—or at least survive—the devastations that befall us during the course of our lives.

8

Ask Questions

Hanani, one of my brothers, came from Judah with some other men, and I questioned them about the Jewish remnant that had survived the exile, and also about Jerusalem.
—Nehemiah 1:2

Ignorance is not bliss; it is just ignorant.

While it is probably true that Nehemiah had never actually been to Jerusalem himself, he likely had some idea that things were not good for those living in Jerusalem. He was, after all, serving right alongside the king of Persia. He had certainly heard reports from Judah and was aware of the vicious and brutal way that King Nebuchadnezzar had destroyed the city when he finally took it into Babylonian control. Nehemiah knew, before asking the question, that the answer might be difficult to hear. Yet he asked the question anyway.

Nehemiah must have understood that hiding from the more difficult and painful realities that surround us is not an effective means of guarding our hearts and souls from pain. While hiding from painful and disturbing issues may, for a time, allow us to continue to live in our blissful state of intentional ignorance, we will still be haunted by the nagging thought that perhaps things are not as good as they seem. This nagging question can do as much to steal our peace and joy as finding out the awful truth in the first place. Furthermore, this intentional ignorance carries with it no hope of healing. As long we don't know, we can't heal.

Now, I am no fan of seeking out sad and devastating stories just for the sake of having a good cry. Sometimes people will say to me, "You have to watch this movie! I cried all the way through it!" This kind of endorsement will guarantee that I do not watch it! The reason is quite simple. There is enough tragedy in the real world, and therefore I don't need to go find fictional tragedy to make me cry! I have dealt with tragedy in my personal and professional life time and again as a pastor, father, son, brother, uncle, and friend. In those roles, I have found more than enough reality to cry about. So, I don't watch sad movies, if I can help it. Once, my wife thought it would be good for me to watch a sad movie with her. I don't even remember the name of the movie, but I vividly remember the teenage girl—a sister, friend, and daughter—dying. I was emotionally devastated—over fiction! That made me angry. I was crying like a child—or like a parent that had just lost a child—when nothing bad had actually happened to me. I was sad and mad!

So, I intentionally don't watch sad movies.

But I also, intentionally, *don't* avoid sad realities. Life is full of them. We all experience them. Avoiding them is not an effective coping mechanism. Instead, it is a form of delusion. We must face the difficult—even the devastating—with our own questions, so that we can achieve our own understanding. Often, this is the first step of working our way out of an identity caught in brokenness.

When I am trying to console someone who has just experienced a devastating loss, I usually start gently and slowly asking questions. As I ask the questions, I watch closely for their response. Almost always, the person whom I am trying to console begins to tell the story, filling in the details to an amazing level of specificity. I find that, when people do this, they are beginning to heal themselves. Telling the story of the tragedy that ended a life, or telling the story of the beauty of the life that is being mourned, allows for healing, catharsis, honor, and questions.

Often, in the middle of telling the story—and often more than once—the person speaking to me will stop and ask a question: "Why did I let them go there?" "Why was the other person so angry?" "Why didn't I see this coming?" "Why didn't she call me?" I obviously do not know the answer to any of these questions, but what I can do is be a comforting presence in the midst of a difficult internal struggle. If no one is there to help shield the blow of these kinds of questions, they run a much higher risk of assuming unhealthy levels of authority and causing destructive levels of confusion by hardening the I-am of brokenness. But with someone there to offset the questions or share in the confusion, the mourner more easily comes to grips with the story at a deeper and more helpful level. Healing can start even at the point of painful discovery.

Alternately, if someone does *not* give specific answers, I change the plan and stop asking questions. Such a person is not ready to deal with the story and simply needs some time to rest in the despair. This is good and acceptable, as long as it doesn't last too long. For this person, I want to practice what is often called the ministry of presence—just be there. Don't let them grieve alone. Don't let them cry alone. Be there, and just sit, cry, pray, listen, get a glass of tea, or whatever; just be there. When someone is suffering, just showing them they are not alone can give great comfort.

Nehemiah was smart enough to know, as he asked these questions, that the answers he would get might be as devastating to him as they were to Hanani, the brother who had just returned from Judah. But he was also mature enough to know that the answers to his questions were the only way to find enlightenment about the world around him.

Honestly, we humans are far too quick to avoid exploring potentially painful issues. We avoid questions that might be controversial or bring answers that are painful. We change the subject when someone who is different than us or thinks differently from us begins to express a view that we may not understand or may not agree with, and we do this simply to avoid the painful reality of what is separating us. The problem is, without the questions, there will be no conversation. Without the conversation, there will be no understanding. Without the understanding, there will be no healing. So, even when you have a real fear of what the answer might be, ask questions. It's the first step to getting past what hurts.

9

Mourn

*When I heard these things, I sat down and wept. For some days
I mourned and fasted and prayed before the God of heaven.*
—Nehemiah 1:4

Those who refuse to mourn never heal.

There is an old belief, especially in the rural American South where I grew up, that men don't cry. While no one ever said these words to me as I was growing up, I nonetheless learned this truth well. I can honestly say that I only saw my stepdad cry once, and that was at his father's funeral, just before they closed the casket. The men I grew up admiring and watching, either close up or from afar, were strong, and as far as I could tell, never cried. This type of strength has its place. The fact that there were few tears with these men gave me the sense that they were strong and could be trusted to protect and guide. I wasn't afraid that they would make some foolish emotional decision that would bring pain to me or anyone around me. They seemed to be in control of their emotions and therefore in control of their world.

But there are limits to how healthy this kind of strength can be.

Now that I am a man who is expected to be strong, I realize that there are some good reasons for controlling emotions. Overt displays of emotion can communicate weakness and instability and leave those who count on you feeling unsafe and insecure. But I also know that not only are there times that showing emotions and shedding tears is appropriate, there are times it would be inappropriate not to cry. The key is found in balance.

When tragedy strikes and brokenness threatens to take over our identity, we must seek out a place of balance. In these moments the dangers are to be found in the extremes. Healing and the return of a proper identity will only be found in a balancing of the sorrow and strength. Neither of these can be ignored without severe consequences.

Despair—Sorrow without Boundaries

Some get caught up in the pain—even the horror—of tragedy and can't seem to find their way out. When this happens, the pain and sorrow can overtake the person's very identity. People caught here begin to identify themselves by their pain. While they may never say it out loud, the message is clear: "I am broken, and I am not going to heal." For any number of reasons, some people just will not or cannot move on. Perhaps they fear that healing is a form of forgetting. Perhaps they simply cannot let go of memorabilia or places that recall a loved one or a tragedy. Perhaps they have just gotten so used to the pain that the mourning has become the only emotion they still feel. No matter the reason, the end result is not healthy.

We have all likely known people who are trapped in boundless and seemingly endless mourning over tragedy. When we are with them, the tragedy or the hurt always becomes the center of the conversation. Joy becomes rare or even absent from their existence, and other people begin to avoid them. In short, these people have become fully identified by their pain, and the despair that defines them begins to isolate them. This cycle of sorrow, left unchecked, can harden the identity of brokenness, like concrete around a person's feet, and leave them drowning in their own hopelessness.

Denial

Denial is very different, but no less damaging, than despair. Those caught in denial refuse to allow their emotions to escape. No one is allowed to see or know of the brokenness, and no one is ever allowed to see the pain that it is causing. Sometimes people in denial will attempt to suppress the pain within—from themselves and others. However, pressing back emotion every time it threatens to rise to the surface is dangerous business. Denial of pain, and therefore refusal to process or move on from pain, often leads to self-medicating through alcohol and drugs. It can also lead to other dangerous and self-destructive behavior. These forms of acting out are often used to mask the pain that is being denied. When the pain threatens to rise up, the acting out is fired up in order to push the pain back down. In the end, this leads to no better a place than despair.

Instead, the real answer is an appropriate level and time of mourning. Nehemiah seemed to understand this.

Let me suggest three actions that can help move the pain out of the center of your identity.

Give It Space

"I sat down and wept" (Neh. 1:4).

Mourning requires some space. It is a thing that needs to happen in our lives, and so it needs to be given *room* to happen. I have watched many people as they have gone through the tragic loss of a loved one. One of the most common reactions I see is simply to stay busy. In the immediate aftermath of the tragic event, they call the funeral home to make arrangements, call the church to arrange the service, and then clean, organize, arrange, and anything else they can think of to stay busy. I don't really discourage this behavior. However, I do make sure that someone is going to look in on them regularly. Because the day will come when there is nothing left to do, and this person will come to a standstill. When that moment arrives, grief will have some space and mourning will happen. No matter what your normal reaction to times like this may be, just remember, eventually you are going to need to give grief some space to happen. Eventually you have to sit down and cry.

Give It Time

"For some days I mourned" (v. 4).

Once you give grief some space, you may notice that it kind of refuses to stay within the boundaries of your schedule. Grief takes time, and the amount of time it takes varies from person to person. I think the best way to handle this is to have flexible boundaries that fit your personality and life. In other words, you cannot, in the face of tragedy, simply say to yourself, "OK, I need to give this grief some time to come out, so I am going to schedule three hours next Tuesday for all of that to take place." Let me say it again, grief refuses to stay within the boundaries of your schedule.

But you can exercise some reasonable controls over the expression of your grief. Start by understanding that it is going to work itself out over a longer period of time. It is not going to be a single three-hour crying session, and then it is over. But it also does not have to be a constant flood of tears that never seem to end. Give yourself a number of days to work through this. We don't really know how many days Nehemiah mourned here, but we do know that his mourning was not measured in minutes or hours; rather it was measured in days. Yours will be the same. Give it time, and then force yourself to move on, all the while understanding that tomorrow you may have to give it a little more time before you move on again. Over time, as you heal and your I-am starts to reset, the grief will take up less space in your life and demand less time.

Give It to God

"I . . . fasted and prayed" (v. 4).

I guess it sounds cliché for a pastor to suggest prayer as a way through mourning and grief, but it's true. Nehemiah understood the power of prayer to comfort and heal in impossible moments. In fact, prayer is often the only power we can bring to a desperate moment in our lives. At the very moment that we realize we cannot, we lean on a God who can! That hope can give healing in the darkest of moments. In prayer, we are reminded that we are more than broken people. We are still, even in the midst of pain, children of God—and our Father can fix anything!

10

Admit Failures

Lᴏʀᴅ, the God of heaven, the great and awesome God, who keeps his covenant of love with those who love him and keep his commandments, let your ear be attentive and your eyes open to hear the prayer your servant is praying before you day and night for your servants, the people of Israel. I confess the sins we Israelites, including myself and my father's family, have committed against you. We have acted very wickedly toward you. We have not obeyed the commands, decrees and laws you gave your servant Moses.

—Nehemiah 1:5–7

Failure admitted can be failure overcome; failure unconfessed leaves me undone.

While it is true that we often face tragedies we did not cause or had no role in, we also face tragedies that are of our own making. When such a tragedy arrives at our doorstep, the logical first step is to admit our failure and seek forgiveness. Nehemiah realized that the fall of Jerusalem was part of a natural pattern of behavior and consequence that one could clearly observe throughout the history of the nation of Israel. Throughout the Old Testament—the record of Israel's history and relationship with God—the Israelites followed God and found blessing, only to then forget God and find struggle. This pattern carried on throughout the existence of the nation. In fact, even before they were an official nation, they struggled in this same way. Before they had kings, they had judges whom God raised up to bring healing and direction when they forgot about him and lost their way. As you read through this historical account, it can be discouraging to see how regularly they forgot to follow God or rejected him altogether. The situation Nehemiah and the Israelites were in at that time was a continuation of that pattern!

In all of ancient history, there were only three kings of Israel that reigned over a unified nation: Saul, David, and Solomon. All three of them had their weaknesses and failings, but all three held the nation together (see 1 and 2 Samuel; 1 Kings 1–11; 1 Chronicles and 2 Chronicles through chapter 9). After Solomon's death, the nation was split into two nations. Israel, the northern nation with its capital in Shechem, had nineteen kings before being overthrown by the Assyrians in 722 BC. Judah, the southern nation with its capital in Jerusalem, had twenty kings and was conquered by the Babylonians in 597 BC. It was subsequently destroyed by Nebuchadnezzar in 586 BC, following an attempted revolt by the final king of Judah, Zedekiah. This time, the Babylonians completely destroyed the city, leaving behind the mess that

Nehemiah was mourning. All of this to say, throughout all of those years and all of those kings, there were only a few godly ones. In the end, the kings who lost sight of the God that gave Israel its meaning and purpose ultimately brought about the destruction of the entire nation.

This same pattern exists in us today.

It is our God who gives us our eternal and pure identity: "See what great love the Father has lavished on us, that we should be called children of God! And that is what we are!" (1 John 3:1). When we forget or reject that identity, we leave ourselves open to attack and failure. In our spiritual lives, we are in a constant struggle with the enemy of our souls. That old snake from the tree in Eden still chases after us. He wants to tear us down, and his tactics haven't changed. He seeks to convince us that we don't need God, we don't understand God, or we are little gods ourselves. No matter what lies he has to tell us to accomplish his goal of separating us from God, he will do it. And when we give in to his lies about who we are, we fall into sin, and that sin has consequences, and sometimes those consequences are devastating.

When we are faced with a moment where the spiritual walls that protect us have been torn down, and we are being emotionally raided and impoverished by our enemies, fears, failures, and tragedies, we must do all we can to get ourselves back to God. He can protect us. He can show us how to regain our proper identity and rebuild our lives to the God-given level of potential that was set in us from the beginning.

The first step in that process is confession.

In the church I pastor, we put this in very simple terms. We simply ask people to remember their ABCs:

Admit – that I have sinned and need forgiveness.

Believe – that God can and will forgive my sins.

Commit – my life and my ways to him from this day forward.

So, on our pathway to moving away from an "I am broken" identity, we have asked questions to promote understanding, mourned to allow for healing, and asked forgiveness to correct the failings of our own heart.

Now we plan to change!

11

Plan Change

Remember the instruction you gave your servant Moses, saying, "If you are unfaithful, I will scatter you among the nations, but if you return to me and obey my commands, then even if your exiled people are at the farthest horizon, I will gather them from there and bring them to the place I have chosen as a dwelling for my Name." They are your servants and your people, whom you redeemed by your great strength and your mighty hand. Lord, let your ear be attentive to the prayer of this your servant and to the prayer of your servants who delight in revering your name. Give your servant success today by granting him favor in the presence of this man.

—Nehemiah 1:8–11

At some point moving on requires change.

The last sentence in this passage, asking for success, shows that a plan was formulating in Nehemiah's mind. He was about to embark on a journey to change the situation in Jerusalem for the better! As healing begins to happen, thinking begins to change. In the midst of brokenness, there is little clarity in thought, little direction, and almost no forward thinking.

Quite honestly, when caught in brokenness, if you can figure out what to cook for a meal and how to cook it, that alone can be a victory. But once healing begins, vision clears and ideas start to flow again.

Nehemiah's time of questioning and mourning gave way to forward thinking. He began to move from "How can I survive this?" to "What can I do about this?" Those who come through tragedy and find healing often take their tragedy and do something with it. Through their pain and destruction, they bring about something life-giving and constructive. I have known numerous families that have started foundations, ministries, or missions after the loss of a child or a spouse. My own niece passed away recently, and her parents set up a mission fund for some global mission work that she was committed to. They then traveled to the mission site to see the work that had been done in her name. Some years ago, a young man in our church died tragically. He had been planning to go with our church to a mission in Guatemala. After his death, his family chose to donate enough money to construct a church in his honor there in the village in Guatemala that he had been planning to visit. Things like this can never make up for tragic loss, but they can give purpose to those left behind.

Even if your brokenness is not connected to the loss of a loved one but rather connected to a failure of your own making, projects and ministries that are life-giving can bring purpose and direction in the most crucial times. Following a personal failure, there is typically a period when everything changes. You may need a new job, a new house, a new career, a new community, sometimes a new life. In these moments of restart, new ideas can give new meaning.

New meaning is born out of a restored I-am.

So, watch for those lights to start coming back on. As the grief and mourning begin to settle and the questions begin to turn to ideas, let the ideas flow. It is wise to move slowly and make sure the healing process has done its full work before you embark on some new career or pick up and move to a new country, but allowing the ideas to flow again can bring a renewed sense of life and can mark the end of the long night of brokenness.

12

Seek Opportunity

I was cupbearer to the king.
—Nehemiah 1:11

You are not where you are by accident.

It is no accident that Nehemiah was where he was. This man, whose heart ached for the restoration of Jerusalem, the city of God, was stationed right alongside the one man in the world who could make that happen. There was literally no one else in the kingdom that could bring together the resources and permissions needed to restore Jerusalem other than King Artaxerxes. And that is who Nehemiah happened to work for.

God always has a plan. While we are busy working our way through grief and brokenness, he patiently waits for us to remember who we are in him. He has always known that these moments would come and that we would be in just the right place to make a difference. While we were questioning why, he was guiding our thoughts, so that we could eventually move from "Why me?" to "How can I . . . ?"

This was his plan all along.

So, let me give you a little insight. God has always had a plan for your life. While he did not cause the painful experiences you have been through, he will use them. He knows where you are and all that you have been through. And he still has a plan for your life. When tragedy strikes and you find yourself in a place of brokenness, remember that you are only here for a time. You are just traveling through. This is not who you are. Your I-am has been set by God your Father, and ultimately, he does not see brokenness and loss, but beauty and promise. Take the time to ask questions, to mourn, and to ask forgiveness, where all of that is appropriate. Through it all, pray. And when God starts sparking new dreams and directions . . . trust him.

PART 3

I AM CALLED

Once the dark night of brokenness is over, you are faced with a new I-am. The problem, at this point, is that most people think that the ending of the night was the point of the story. But it was not and is not. We think this way because it's how we have been conditioned to think. Entertainment media, so pervasive in our world, has taught us to get to know a character, watch them fall into some type of tragedy, struggle through it, overcome it, and then ride off into the sunset.

Have you ever asked yourself what those people do the next morning? Such simple questions can help us think past the shallow endings presented by our surface culture. Think about it: Do the gladiators ever need to take out the trash when they get home? Do the great warriors in the movies go home and do the dishes? While their story ends with a great party and celebration, your story continues the next morning, when you need to get up and clean up everyone's celebratory mess. In other words, there is life after brokenness, but that isn't a promise of a beautiful ending; it is the promise of a new beginning.

So, your story moves on, and you are no longer identified by your brokenness. Instead, you have a purpose, a goal, a calling. God has strategically placed you right where you are, and he has work for you to do. Now that you are healed—or at least healing—from your grief, you can stop identifying as "I am broken" and start identifying as "I am called." But this calling will require something—perhaps everything—from you.

It's time to move on.

13

Make a Plan

In the month of Nisan in the twentieth year of King Artaxerxes,
when wine was brought for him, I took the wine and gave it to
the king. I had not been sad in his presence before.
—Nehemiah 2:1

All great outcomes begin with a simple plan.

Nehemiah needed to take steps to accomplish what God had put on his heart to do for Jerusalem. But nothing in his situation had changed. This is an important lesson that must be learned by everyone who feels a calling to some purpose or mission. Just because you are called doesn't mean everything will naturally fall into place. Calling doesn't circumvent work and planning. An old adage says that every overnight success was many years in the making. This is true. We become aware of success only after it has been achieved. What we often don't hear about is the many days, months, even years that were spent planning and working the plan in order to finally arrive at "overnight" success.

Sitting in his room mourning and praying, Nehemiah began to formulate a plan. Once his mind cleared from the mourning, he focused on the plans that God was birthing in his heart. He wondered how this vision could be brought about. He dreamed about a different Jerusalem, a rebuilt Jerusalem. His dreams caused him to question how he could accomplish such a huge task. This must have seemed virtually impossible to him as he lifted above the fog of his sorrow. And yet, perhaps, if God was in it, somehow, it could work out!

Let me suggest a few ideas that may have informed Nehemiah's thinking during the time between his mournful prayers and his fateful moment with the king.

Organize Your Steps

Dreams are great. But they don't become reality without structure. As I write this, I am at a rented lake house so that I can focus. I literally just ordered a pizza, and the kid that delivered it walked to the door and said to me, "It's my dream to one day live on the lake!" I have to be honest, there was a time in my life when that was one of my dreams as well. The difference between that kid and me is about thirty years of life experience. So I wanted to sit him down and talk to him about the steps he would need to take in order to achieve his dream of living on the lake. It is actually an achievable dream, especially if you are currently only in your late teens or early twenties. To one day live on the lake, you would need to do the following:

1. Start saving money now.
2. Further your education to increase your income.
3. Work hard at your chosen career in order to achieve higher levels of success—and therefore higher levels of income.
4. Keep watching for opportunity.

Those four simple steps, if they are carefully adhered to, would virtually guarantee that the kid who delivered my pizza could one day live on this lake.

The problem is that most people never actually sit down and make a workable plan. People have great hope, but lack realistic plans. That is why so much money can be made through lottery ticket sales. Everyone hopes that they will win the lottery, but few are making great plans so that they won't *need* to play the lottery. I often point out to people that you rarely see someone step out of a limo to buy lottery tickets. The guy in the limo knows that, with a good plan, he has infinitely better odds of success than with one cheap ticket.

So, make a plan. Organize some beginning steps. With the ultimate end in mind, ask yourself some simple questions: Where should I start? Who should I talk to? Who can help me? What do I need? Once you have processed these questions, then put together the first three to five steps you need to take in order to get things started.

Plan Your Reactions

Now, dreams are great, but not everyone will see your dream as a good idea. People will have varying reactions to your calling. Some will dismiss you entirely. Some will kindly and politely attempt to seem interested, only to walk away and never think about your calling again. But some will choose to support you. You need to be ready for whatever reaction you could possibly get. Your risks in this area may not be that great, but in some instances, the cost of a poor reaction can be very hard to overcome.

In Nehemiah's case, the risk of a poor reaction from the king was rather high. He was the king's cupbearer. Among other things, if the king wanted some wine, Nehemiah was to get the wine, sip it first to be certain it was not poisoned, and then give the cup to the king. He was the king's bartender. While it is normal and acceptable for the drinker to share disappointments and concerns with the bartender, it is not so normal and acceptable for the bartender to start whining to the customers. In the same way, Nehemiah was there to bring comfort and enjoyment to the king. He had no right to bother the king with his own sadness or concerns. It was no mistake that he had "not been sad in his presence before" (Neh. 2:1). If the cupbearer was always sad before the king, there were only two likely outcomes: either the cupbearer would be replaced and become unemployed, or the cupbearer would be executed for messing up the king's mood! So, Nehemiah was taking a huge risk to bring up his own concerns. But he had done his homework: he had prepared how to respond to how the king reacted to him.

Keep in mind that there is nothing fake or disingenuous about this. Preparing yourself to have a proper response to someone else's reaction to your mood is wise and kind.

Years ago, I had a parishioner confess something to me that was shocking to say the least. Fortunately, as God would have it, the Holy Spirit had warned me ahead of time about the confession I was going to hear. Since I was prepared for the confession, I was able to manage my reaction and respond gently and kindly. Had I not been prepared I may have reacted poorly and caused a level of hurt and anger toward the church that would have taken years to heal. Being prepared for the reaction of other people to your plans is absolutely wise and honest.

Set Your Timeframe

Dreams are great, but if you never take the first step toward achieving them, they won't become reality. A great plan is not a great plan until it is put into action. It is only a wasted piece of paper. Dreams require plans, and plans require first steps. So, get the plan together, and then set a date for taking that first leap into the unknown. And know this: the first step is usually the hardest. It's frightening. Sometimes it's downright terrifying! But it is also revealing and sometimes rewarding. At the very least, your first step will let you know how another person feels about your plan. At the very best, it will launch you forward into your new normal. And once that first step is taken, the others tend to come more easily and naturally, until one day you look back and it all makes perfect sense. On that day, you think to yourself, "What was I so afraid of? That was obviously the right thing to do!"

14

Remember Your Place

So the king asked me, "Why does your face look so sad when are not ill? This can be nothing but sadness of heart." I was very much afraid, but I said to the king, "May the king live forever! Why should my face not look sad when the city where my ancestors are buried lies in ruins, and its gates have been destroyed by fire?"

—Nehemiah 2:2–3

"I am called" does not mean "I am king"!

It is refreshing to read about Nehemiah's approach to King Artaxerxes. Nehemiah knew what God had called him to do, but he still honored the king and understood his own place in the king's court. He remembered that, in the king's presence, he had no legal right or protection to show sadness or disappointment over the way a certain city or people group under the king's rule had been treated. This was not an elected president, and Nehemiah had no constitutional right to question him. This was the king, and no one under his authority had the right to question him without the king specifically granting that right. In this instance, the "bartender" was planning to question the king. No wonder Nehemiah was "very much afraid" (Neh. 2:2).

Now, most of us don't live in that kind of world (thank God!). There are very few, if any, moments in our lives when we should be "very much afraid" to show our emotions or speak our minds. However, that does not mean that we should not remain very conscious of our place when we do so. While we may not answer to a king, we likely have bosses and other authority figures whose help or permission we will need to actually accomplish something in our lives. All of us answer to someone, and when addressing that someone, it is good to remember our place.

Today, for some people, I am one of those authority figures. I now know that I can strike instant fear into the heart of a church staff person simply by walking up to their desk and saying, "Hey, take a walk with me." Without intent to cause fear, I have watched some of them lose the color in their faces after I've said that. It was almost never a negative walk (though certainly some have been set free to pursue God's best for their lives during one of those walks), but the very thought of such a walk was still frightening to them. What they may not have realized is that I have had some of the same experiences in my life. For example, when my phone rings, and I look down to see that it is the General Superintendent (GS) of our denomination, my heart always skips a beat, even though I have never had a negative or difficult conversation with any of our GSs. Just knowing that they have the authority to fire me and put an end to my career causes me to answer the phone quickly and politely—because I know my place!

Remembering your place is always helpful, no matter what level of success you may achieve. And in the end, we are all servants of God our Father. Even Jesus practiced this and gave us the example we should follow. The apostle Paul tells us to "have the same mindset as Christ Jesus: Who, being in very nature God, did not consider equality with God something to be used to his own advantage; rather, he made himself nothing by taking the very nature of a servant, being made in human likeness. And being found in appearance as a man, he humbled himself by becoming obedient to death—even death on a cross" (Phil. 2:5–8). This is Jesus whom Paul was talking about—God the Son, part of the Holy Trinity, Savior of the world—and yet he chose to take a lower place. He did this even though, as the apostle pointed out, "at the name of Jesus every knee should bow, in heaven and on earth and under the earth, and every tongue acknowledge that Jesus Christ is Lord, to the glory of God the Father" (Phil. 2:10–11).

Remember that you are inviting people to join you on the journey you believe that God has called you to. You do not have the right to demand that they follow you simply because of your call. Instead you have the opportunity to have them walk alongside you as you follow your call. You are not king; you are called. That calling, once you accept it, is one of the most important things in your life, but it is yours and no one else is required to come along with you. So, take up the attitude of Christ, the attitude of a servant, and present your calling to others—without demanding that they bow to your preferences—and God the Holy Spirit will take care of the rest.

15

Ask God, Then Ask People

The king said to me, "What is it you want?" Then I prayed to the God of heaven, and I answered the king, "If it pleases the king and if your servant has found favor in his sight, let him send me to the city in Judah where my ancestors are buried so that I can rebuild it."

—Nehemiah 2:4–5

When someone asks what it is you want, know the answer!

Can you imagine if this moment came, and the king asked Nehemiah "What is it you want?" and Nehemiah replied by saying, "You know, king, I'm not sure. I actually didn't think I would get this far, and I haven't really thought this all the way through. The situation in Jerusalem just bugs me."

While this might seem silly to read, the reality is that some people jump into conversations with people who have much to offer them, without knowing what they would want if they were given the opportunity to ask. This is poor planning. You must think through what outcome you are looking for before launching into a conversation with anyone in authority. When

God opens the door for me to meet with someone I want to learn from, I spend more time preparing for the meeting than I do in the meeting itself. I try to think through the questions that would be most helpful to me. I consider how I would react to certain responses or reactions from them. I want to be prepared to get the most out of the meeting that I possibly can. I try never to go into a meeting like that without knowing the outcomes I am looking for.

Nehemiah knew what he wanted. But the key point is this part of the passage: "The king said to me, "'What is it you want?' Then I prayed to the God of heaven" (Neh. 2:4). Before answering the king, Nehemiah prayed.

Prayer is one of the great missing elements in much of our planning. We seem to accept a calling from God and then forget to include him in planning for the launch of our calling. This is a mistake.

The Vision Was Birthed in Prayer

Nehemiah's vision was birthed in his time of mourning, fasting, and praying. As God was healing Nehemiah's heart, he was also birthing Nehemiah's vision for repairing Jerusalem. Honestly, if you think back and try to remember, I believe you will find that many of your own visions and perhaps all of your callings were birthed in times of concerted, focused prayer. When we are quiet before God, the Holy Spirit speaks to us and births within us the dreams and visions that will ultimately define us. Prayer changes things by changing me first.

The Vision Was Bathed in Prayer

I don't think we even need to have a verse to tell us that Nehemiah had been praying nonstop for this vision since he received it from the Holy Spirit. And don't think for one minute he hadn't been praying nonstop about this conversation with the king—one that might end with his execution, his rejection, or his empowerment. That's a big conversation! We need to bathe our visions in prayer all along the way. Constant prayer keeps us in right relationship with God and keeps our spirit open to direction from God as we work out his call on our life. Bathing the entire process in prayer is absolutely required.

The Vision Was Presented with Prayer

In that one moment between the king's question and Nehemiah's answer, Nehemiah prayed. Even in the moment, we need to be people of active prayer. Quite often, I will find myself begging God for the exact right word at the exact right moment in important or difficult conversations. When we do this, we remind ourselves of our need for the guidance of the Holy Spirit, and our reliance on his leading and sustaining power. When it has got to be right, it should be prayed for, right up to the second the words fall out of our mouths.

The Vision Is Nurtured through Prayer

As we go through the rest of this account from Nehemiah, we will find him in a constant attitude of prayer. We find him praying for protection, understanding, and direction. All the way through the process, Nehemiah kept praying.

The temptation for many of us is to neglect prayer once we are in the heat of the work. We received the calling through prayer, and we certainly launched it with a lot of prayer, but now that it is going well and has become our fulltime job, we tend to stop praying and just keep working. This is a mistake. The guidance that we so obviously relied on in the beginning is still needed in the midst of the work. In fact, it is here, in the heat of battle, that we need prayer so desperately. Pastor Aaron Rummage has worked with us at New Life Church for almost twenty years now. Both of us have prayed a simple prayer for twenty years: "Dear God, don't let us screw this up!" I have to admit that there have been times when I would get so busy or distracted that I forgot, for a time, to keep praying that humble little prayer. But somehow, along the way, the Holy Spirit would always have someone bring it back up and remind me. That someone has often been Pastor Aaron, and that means the world to me. This prayer has certainly guarded me—and us—from mistakes that could have screwed the whole thing up.

16

Know Your Needs

Then the king, with the queen sitting beside him, asked me, "How long will your journey take, and when will you get back?" It pleased the king to send me; so I set a time. I also said to him, "If it pleases the king, may I have letters to the governors of Trans-Euphrates, so that they will provide me safe-conduct until I arrive in Judah? And may I have a letter to Asaph, keeper of the royal park, so he will give me timber to make beams for the gates of the citadel by the temple and for the city wall and for the residence I will occupy?" And because the gracious hand of my God was upon me, the king granted my requests.

—Nehemiah 2:6–8

An unresourced plan is a failed plan.

Notice that even more consideration had gone into this plan since its inception during Nehemiah's time of mourning. He had thought this thing through! Now it's your turn. When setting out to accomplish any goal that is part of the calling God has placed on your life you must take the time to consider all that will be needed to accomplish that goal. The list will likely be long, and the process may seem tedious, but it is absolutely necessary that you think through what your needs will be.

Too many people jump into a calling with the same attitude with which they jump into a relationship: "All we need is love, and we will be fine!" (Gag!) But even with love and relationships, this is not a true statement. Let's explore it for just a moment. When I fell in love with my wife, Tina, back when we were teenagers, it all seemed so simple. But then we decided to get married, and that was going to require love and a lot more! She needed a dress, and I needed a tux. We had to work through the guest list, get premarital counseling from our pastor, work out dates, plan for food, music, candles, flowers, someone to work lights and sound, someone to make the program, people to pass out the program, people to be our bridesmaids and groomsmen—and they also needed dresses and tuxes. There had to be birdseed to throw on our way out and a cake to cut at the reception. And then there was the honeymoon. We needed airline tickets (and I had never been on an airplane before, so courage was needed!), a hotel room, transportation to and from the airport, some idea of food, we needed to save some money to take with us, we needed to pack and get to everything we had planned on time. And then when we came back from the honeymoon, we had to live somewhere . . . and then . . . kids?!

You get it, right? That little thing called love includes a really long list of needs along the way. Now, there was no way

I could have known all the needs I would have for our entire marriage. Fortunately, that isn't what is required. But in order to make a given calling work, you do have to look at each stage of development of that calling and carefully figure out what your needs are going to be as you go forward.

Nehemiah had already thought all of this through. Had he not thought to ask for letters for safe passage, he and his traveling party may have been attacked and killed before ever reaching Jerusalem. Had he not thought to ask for a letter to the keeper of the forest, he would have arrived and not had the resources necessary to accomplish the task at hand, and that would have certainly cost him the support he so desperately needed from the already existing residents of Jerusalem. Why would they follow an unprepared leader?

How you come up with these lists of needs is a process that is fairly unique to each person. In my case, I take a walk through the plan multiple times in my mind before I even start working on the plan in order to consider what I might need at each stage. If it is possible for me to physically walk through the given site or building where my plan is to play out, that is even better. I walked into the woods before our church building was built, because I knew basically where everything would eventually be. I stood on the stage in my mind in order to consider what might be needed, in case we had forgotten something. Each time I do this type of planning, I make lists. Over time, I can compile the lists, and from there I can arrive at an overall list of needs and a pretty accurate cost that I will face once it's all done. However you choose to assess your needs, do it. Don't let yourself be caught standing in the presence of the one person who can make your calling work, without a clue as to what you might need and could ask for.

17

Set Your Goals

So I went to the governors of Trans-Euphrates and gave them the king's letters. The king had also sent army officers and cavalry with me.

—Nehemiah 2:9

Launching starts with leaving.

At some point in every great calling there is a moment of leaving. This moment can be really exciting for some and really frightening for others. Nehemiah wrote, "It pleased the king to send me; so I set a time" (Neh. 2:6). After he had worked his plan as much as he could from the capital, he launched out into the unknown. This is where the risks got real. Before, Nehemiah had been making plans and gathering letters, but then he had to physically leave the city he had likely lived in his entire life to set out for a place he had never been to in order to accomplish something that he had never done before. He was a cupbearer, not a contractor, but there he was setting out, navigating dangerous political landscapes, and preparing to lead a massive, city-wide infrastructure project. Such days can test a person's faith.

First steps are just difficult. There is really no way around it. Anytime we launch out into the unknown, there is going to be fear and risk involved. One day we may look back and realize how silly we were to worry about those risks, but this is not that day. When Tina and I were called to pastor the church we now serve, we had to move from North Carolina, where we had both lived for our entire lives, to Maryland. Now, for many people, I suppose, that may not seem like such a risk. But I knew I was going to be a Carolina boy for the rest of my life. I didn't know if Marylanders would appreciate my preaching style, accept my family, or respond to my leadership.

Looking back on it, I had nothing to worry about. These are good people and this is a good place to live. But at the time it was tough. I can remember loading up the truck and pulling out of our driveway for the last time, headed up to Maryland. It was more than a little frightening. Each time I have had to launch out into an unknown area of leadership or work, I have had that same knot in my stomach. Often when people ask me at the start of a new endeavor, "You think this will work?" I respond with, "Ask me again in ten years, and I will let you know!" It's the only answer I know to that question, especially when we are on the front end of something we have never done before.

But fear or not, you have to take that first step. As Nehemiah headed out of the capital city that day, what thoughts must have been going through his mind? Here he was, a servant, a bartender for the king, and now leading a mission to rebuild his ancestral home. He was carrying letters from the king, and as a bonus, the king had thrown in army officers and cavalry to join him. That's a big leap in responsibility for a bartender! But God does things like that.

He takes people who are willing and turns them into people who are able.

And that is what he will do with you as well.

So, make your plans, remember your place, pray a lot, figure out what you are going to need, and then get this thing moving! If God is in it, it's going to be awesome!

PART 4

I AM EMPOWERED

As Nehemiah entered Jerusalem, he arrived as a fully empowered leader with all of the permissions and resources he would need to accomplish the task at hand. I can just imagine him riding into the city with his royal garb and surrounded by the army officers and the king's cavalry. For the inhabitants of this besieged city, it must have been quite a spectacle.

But Nehemiah did not ride into the city and immediately announce his plans and intentions. Just because someone has permission and the necessary resources doesn't mean they have the local support required to ultimately accomplish the goal. Nehemiah had ancestral history in Jerusalem, but he was not from there. There was much work to be done before the construction work could begin.

Too many leaders believe that, having the permission of some important official and the resources and ability to accomplish some task, they can simply get started and everyone else will fall into line behind them. This is usually not the case. Even when you have come to help improve people's lives, you cannot do your work until they *agree* to have their lives improved and to let you be the one to lead them there. No amount of resources or bureaucratic permissions can overcome a lack of local buy-in. So, Nehemiah set out to turn the empowerment he had brought from the king into the engagement of the people he had been called to help.

18

Imagine Success

I went to Jerusalem, and after staying there three days I set out during the night with a few others. I had not told anyone what my God had put in my heart to do for Jerusalem. There were no mounts with me except the one I was riding on. By night I went out through the Valley Gate toward the Jackal Well and the Dung Gate, examining the walls of Jerusalem, which had been broken down, and its gates, which had been destroyed by fire. Then I moved on toward the Fountain Gate and the King's Pool, but there was not enough room for my mount to get through; so I went up the valley by night, examining the wall. Finally, I turned back and reentered through the Valley Gate. The officials did not know where I had gone or what I was doing, because as yet I had said nothing to the Jews or the priests or nobles or officials or any others who would be doing the work.

—Nehemiah 2:11–16

Paint with your mind before ever picking up a paintbrush. Nehemiah's arrival in the city of Jerusalem must have caused quite a stir. Everyone would have known that some important official had come to town, but no one was exactly sure why he was there. He intentionally did not share his plans with any of the city officials. Instead, he just spent three days getting a feel for what the city was like and getting to know them. During that time, I imagine that he talked with leaders and discussed what they were worried about. Then, on the third night, he quietly set out with a few of his own men and toured the city walls. He specifically noted where the destruction was worst and what would need to be done. As he rode around the city that night, he was clearly mapping out the work that would lie ahead of him. In his mind's eye, he was envisioning what the finished product would look like.

This first step of imagining success is often overlooked in our rush to get started with our plan and get the job done. But when we skip this step, we fail to see areas that need special attention or areas that can give spectacular results. In this first phase of envisioning, we see *what could be* through a firsthand viewing of *what already is*. While Nehemiah had certainly seen what a city wall should look like and would have been familiar with this type of structure, that night he saw the specific landscape of Jerusalem. As he rode around the perimeter of the city, over hills and through valleys, he realized that rebuilding the wall would require precise, skilled labor. The scope of the work became clear to him for the first time. While he had heard plenty about Jerusalem from others, this was a chance to actually see what he was up against. Add to all of this the scale of the destruction and the fact that there were places he couldn't even get his horse through because of the piles of debris that were blocking the way.

Soon Nehemiah would need to stand before the people of the city and convince them to work with him to accomplish the project he had been sent to complete and rebuild the walls of this once-great city. But before he could do that, he needed that firsthand look at everything they would have to work on. Having journeyed around the wall himself, he could prepare himself for the moment when he had to speak to the leaders and ask them to join him. He had gained a sense of where these officials all lived and how vulnerable their houses and properties were to invasion due to the broken-down walls. He could more knowledgably appeal to their need to protect and guard their families, as well as to their desire to rebuild the city of their ancestors. He also had developed an understanding of them as people. In the end this project was about them. This was not his city, nor would it ever really be his city. In fact, after the work on the wall was completed, he would return to the capital city of Babylon and not return to Jerusalem until years later. As an outsider, he needed to win the hearts of the ones who would be doing the work.

Whenever you face a new project, take the time to imagine the end result before you start the work. Before the first stroke of a paintbrush, an artist has already seen in his mind's eye what the final product will be. Along the way there may be alterations, improvements, or improvisations, but the final product will look strikingly similar to what was in the mind of the artist before he or she started. This same truth should apply to your life calling. When you believe you have a call from God to accomplish a particular task, take the time to imagine it before you put your hands to doing it. Take a moment and revel in the beauty of the completed project as it exists already in your imagination. In doing this, you will make a better final product, and you will better prepare yourself for the task of bringing others on board.

19

Engage Influencers

Then I said to them, "You see the trouble we are in: Jerusalem lies in ruins, and its gates have been burned with fire. Come, let us rebuild the wall of Jerusalem, and we will no longer be in disgrace." I also told them about the gracious hand of my God on me and what the king had said to me. They replied, "Let us start rebuilding." So they began this good work.
—Nehemiah 2:17–18

Great work requires full buy-in from fully invested people. Nehemiah faced the task of standing before the people of Jerusalem and convincing them to move forward with the rebuilding of their city. While Nehemiah's announcement seemed to go extremely well, don't let the seeming ease cause you to expect such early and quick buy-in when you present your own new plans. This type of quick, unanimous agreement is extremely rare. It is possible that the residents of Jerusalem were so tired and frustrated from all the invaders who troubled their city that they were just ready to settle in and follow anyone with a plan and some resources. Or, it could be that Nehemiah just didn't tell the entire story of this town hall meeting where he, as the outsider, announced that he had plans that the lifelong residents needed to follow. Whatever the case, be prepared for more push back than Nehemiah apparently received when you present your God-given call to the people God called you to. People give many reasons for not wanting to follow a God-called leader. Let's take a look at just a few and consider how to overcome them.

Apathy

While the residents of Jerusalem seem to have signed on very quickly with Nehemiah's plan, they had spent their entire lives in at least some level of apathy. Jerusalem was destroyed by Nebuchadnezzar's army in the year 587 BC and Nehemiah arrived around 430 BC. So, for approximately 150 years, the residents of Jerusalem had not pulled themselves together to fix this wall on their own. They had, in fact, left heaps of rubble lying around, to the degree that Nehemiah could not freely navigate his horse around the remnants of the entire wall. These were people who had, for some reason, not fixed the problem themselves. I can just hear them saying, "Here comes this rich guy from the king who lives far away, and we are just supposed to listen to him?" This is how many groups would—and do—react.

Truth is that sometimes the Holy Spirit gives you a moment where people are so ready for change that they will sign on quickly with the change you are bringing. However, those times are not the norm. For a group of people who have not experienced change in a long time, the idea of investing heavily in some new project may not be all that appealing. You must help them see the final goal. The imagination exercise in the last section is useful here. In order to motivate the people God has called you to, you must be able to paint a picture of their future that is so compelling that it becomes worth all the work and pain of change. Only then will they join you. But once they do join in, they can find the same meaning and fulfillment that you have already experienced, and improve their situation in the process!

Familiarity

When you are a newly arrived and empowered leader, it is important to learn everything you can to help you understand the people you have come to lead. Remember that there is a whole back story that you may know nothing about yet. Remember how, during his tour of the wall, Nehemiah found that "there was not enough room for my mount to get through" (Neh. 2:14). In my mind's eye, Nehemiah encountered a place where, over the previous century and a half, the rubble and debris had only been cleared away enough for a single person to walk through. Why had no one thought it important to clean that up or make more room? There is a story there that we are not told, but that, in that moment, could matter to a leader like Nehemiah. As you "tour the walls" of your calling, look for places that make you ask "Why?" Then ask! The stories you get will help inform you as to how to proceed and may help you avoid unnecessary conflict.

I am a pastor. When I took over at my first church as a solo pastor, I was greeted with a long list of things that needed to be changed or upgraded in the church's physical building. God blessed, and within the first two years of being there, we were able to complete almost the entire list. This meant that everything had changed. Every wall had been painted, and every floor covering had been replaced. Everything was new and different. Well, almost everything. There was this one chapel. It was actually just a rather small room that could seat maybe twenty-five people. It was called the Peggy Wall Memorial Chapel. I didn't touch that room. Peggy Wall was the wife of a beloved former pastor. She had died of cancer while she and her husband pastored the church, and their children had stayed in the area even after their father remarried and took another church in another town. He had pastored there long before I had arrived, but within this very stable congregation, almost everyone still remembered Peggy Wall. So I didn't change that room. The change would not have been worth the conflict and angst it would have caused, so I left it alone. Shortly after all of this work was done, the pastor whom I had followed into this church brought his family and attended services with us. They had pastored here for a number of years and raised their children in this church. I could see that the family was struggling with all of the changes that had taken place. Then I saw their daughter suddenly run up to her brother and say, "Come here! They haven't changed this!" and the two of them ran into the chapel and stayed there for quite a while.

As an empowered leader, you must understand the emotional ties that people make to things. Those things may be of no real value in the completion of your mission, but they have an immeasurable value to the people you are leading. Take the time to know those stories so that you will know what you are dealing with before it's too late. It may be that you must make the change anyway. If so, at least you will know where to expect the anger and hurt, and you can work in advance to minimize it. But it also may be that this thing, this story, does not have to be affected. While it has no real value to your progress, it also will not hinder your progress. In those cases, leave it alone. Then those who get a little freaked out from all the change can run over and sit in the chapel for a while!

"You ain't from here!"

Now, I must admit, I am surprised that this accusation seems to be missing from Nehemiah's account. It may be that the cultural norms of the day gave so much authority to the representative of the king that no one was surprised, shocked, or hesitant to follow this new guy. But our culture is not generally like that. Especially in smaller towns or organizations, generational investment matters. By this I mean that people who have lived or worked together in the same community, church, business, or organization for years create a very distinct culture that they see as the norm. There may have been little to no thought put into the cultural expectations that have been created, but they are nonetheless there. As a newly empowered leader from the outside, you must simply accept the fact that your lack of generational investment is going to weaken your standing in the minds of some people. Our next few chapters will provide guidance for overcoming this objection.

In the end, there can be any number of reasons that a group God sent you to work with fails to buy into your God-given call. No amount of empowerment from headquarters will overcome a lack of buy-in on the ground. As the empowered leader, you must find ways to bring the locals on board. Only when they willingly join in can you experience that wonderful moment that seemed to come so easily for Nehemiah here: "So they began this good work!" (v. 18).

20

Entrust Authority

*Eliashib the high priest and his fellow priests went to work
and rebuilt the Sheep Gate.*
—Nehemiah 3:1

Buy-in, without entrusted authority, is short-lived.

Over and over again throughout chapter 3 of Nehemiah,
we are told about the people who repaired certain sections
of the wall. Nehemiah had chosen, either by his own wisdom
or the wisdom of the local leaders who bought into the vision
with him, to empower people to rebuild the walls near their
own homes and businesses.

This was simply brilliant.

Nehemiah clearly realized that his work was to empower,
not to do. He did not bring in contractors from the capital or
workers from the neighboring cities and pay them to do the
work. No, he gave authority to the people who were closest
to the problem so that they could fix it. This transformed two
potential problems into advantages.

Engaged Familiarity

The same thing identified as a problem in the last chapter—familiarity—can be harnessed to become an asset. When you empower the people who live closest to the problem you are trying to fix, you engage the ones who are most familiar with the problem. These people grew up climbing over the debris of this former wall. They walked past it every day. They knew where the foundations were, and they knew which of the older foundations could be trusted and which needed to be rebuilt. They knew where to find the old stockpiles of stones that came out of the original wall that could be reused to rebuild. In short, once they bought in, their familiarity with the situation became a very real asset to the project. Quite honestly, some of them had likely wanted to do this work their entire lives, but no one had ever given them permission to move forward.

Permission is a powerful thing when handed to someone who cares.

As an empowered leader, you must be confident enough to be generous with the authority you have been given. You may be the one who is empowered, but you are not always the one who is informed. You, like Nehemiah, may not even be from here. You don't know the right move or the right thing to do. But someone does. Someone has been just waiting to be given the permission and authority to fix this problem. If you can find that someone and give that authority, you will be amazed at the results!

Ensured Quality

When someone is working on their own project, they are far more careful to see that it is done right. These people were building the wall they would rely on to protect them. They were not about to take shortcuts that would leave them and their families vulnerable to attack. They had lived like that for too long. Here was their chance to see to it that those invaders could no longer swoop in and steal the fruits of their labors. When you bring in workers from the outside, if it's a good company with good leadership, you may get quality. But when you empower workers from the inside to improve the place they live in, you pretty much guarantee quality work.

Local work and local leadership also builds local community. When people work together to build something in their community, they build bonds and history together that are not easily broken or lost. When I was a child, my stepdad was a construction superintendent. I vividly remember him overseeing the construction of First Presbyterian Church in downtown Kannapolis, North Carolina. We all went out to watch when they brought the crane to the site to set the steeple in place. That had to be forty years ago. To this day, if I find myself driving down in that section, I cannot help but glance over at that steeple. It may not be the most beautiful church in town, nor is it the most impressive. But it means something to me. I never forgot that feeling. Therefore, whenever we have a building project in our church these days, I always want local companies to do the work. I know how those workers feel about the buildings they put up and the pride they hold onto for the rest of their lives over being part of a project. But I also know that the same pride will run through their children. I have never entered First Presbyterian Church in Kannapolis that I can recall. Never been to church there; never been to a meeting there; and still somehow I am connected there. That is the power of entrusted authority.

21

Empower Family

*Jedaiah son of Harumaph made repairs opposite his house,
and Hattush son of Hashabneiah made repairs next to him.*
—Nehemiah 3:10

Projects come and go, but family is forever.

Not only did Nehemiah give permission and authority to local individuals and groups like the priests, he also empowered families to do the work next to their own houses. This is an extension of the last point, but it is a distinct extension: anytime that you as a leader can empower *family* in the completion of a project, especially a community project, you will create a synergy that has few equals. Family projects add more than just progress to your mission, they add meaning.

It's not lost on anyone who attends the church I pastor that family is an important part of our leadership structure. My wife and two of my three sons work together with me at the church. They don't do this because daddy "got them a job in the family business." They do it because it's what our family has always done. From the time our sons were born, they were in church with Tina and me. In fact, each of them attended their first church service within their first week of life. As Tina and I served in the church in North Carolina and now in our current church in Maryland, we always brought them along with us. When they were old enough, they began helping in the church. They would serve in children's church, help with community projects, and sing in choirs; it was just who we were. We did church as a family. So when they grew up and began to consider careers, the church was an obvious choice. Once they proved their value to the organization, they were hired.

Now, you may wonder about our leadership structure with all of those Hilsons working at one church. Truth is, we have a very large staff, so it all just blends in. Furthermore, the family ties within our staff are not limited to people with my last name. We actually have a standard practice of allowing campus pastors to hire their spouses in well-defined, structured roles, just like we hired Tina all those years ago in a well-defined, structured role that could easily be evaluated by someone other than me. So, today, New Life Church is deeply committed to families. We are one. Sometimes literally!

When you engage families in your calling, you end up with this kind of commitment. Work becomes more than just work, more even than just a career; it becomes part of your identity. We are church people. We are restaurant people. We are (add your family identifier here). When this is done well and carefully managed, it is truly powerful. When Nehemiah saw this wall completed, there were families that stood together and proudly watched the dedication of the wall they had built. None of them would ever forget the power and pride of that moment. Whenever possible, empower family.

It is true that there can be very serious dangers in family-run organizations. Groupthink, inability to let go of legacy programs and policies that no longer work, and relational fallout within the central family can all cause great damage to an organization that is family centered and family run. So, if this is where your calling seems to be headed, take the time to sit down with the family members that will serve alongside you and the organization leaders with authority over you and clearly articulate where boundaries exist and what consequences will be incurred by failing to maintain those boundaries.

Navigating this is not always easy or comfortable, but it is absolutely necessary. We have had to make it painfully clear that the strength and progress of our church would take precedence over a family member's job. We will not sacrifice the church to save anyone's feelings. Our mission is our mission, and our commitment to family cannot be allowed to thwart that. So, I believe in working alongside family members and see it as powerful and effective. But I also see, understand, and protect against its downsides. You will do well to consider all of that early on and, from the beginning, set the boundaries and expectations with family members and organizational leadership structures.

22

Ensure Fairness

Now the men and their wives raised a great outcry against their fellow Jews. Some were saying, "We and our sons and daughters are numerous; in order for us to eat and stay alive, we must get grain." Others were saying, "We are mortgaging our fields, our vineyards and our homes to get grain during the famine." Still others were saying, "We have had to borrow money to pay the king's tax on our fields and vineyards. Although we are of the same flesh and blood as our fellow Jews and though our children are as good as theirs, yet we have to subject our sons and daughters to slavery. Some of our daughters have already been enslaved, but we are powerless, because our fields and our vineyards belong to others." When I heard their outcry and these charges I was very angry.
—Nehemiah 5:1–6

Great progress must ensure progress for everyone.

As Nehemiah placed all of his attention on the construction of the walls around Jerusalem, there were problems rumbling just beneath the surface. Some of the less wealthy inhabitants of Jerusalem were struggling to make their bills and feed their families. Not unlike today, this provided a profitable opportunity for those who did have money. Loans were being given, interest was being charged, and the wealthy were getting wealthier, while the poor were slipping further into poverty.

When the complaints of the city's poor finally reached Nehemiah, he was outraged by the practices the wealthier inhabitants were engaging in. Not only were families being subjected to high levels of debt, in many cases, they were losing their property and even being forced to sell their children into slavery. In the face of this injustice, Nehemiah chose to take action. The steps he took are instructive for us even today.

Call Out Injustice

I pondered them in my mind and then accused the nobles and officials. I told them, "You are charging your own people interest!" So I called together a large meeting to deal with them and said: "As far as possible, we have bought back our fellow Jews who were sold to the Gentiles. Now you are selling your own people, only for them to be sold back to us!" They kept quiet, because they could find nothing to say (Neh. 5:7–8).

Roaches scurry and hide only when the lights are turned on. Likewise, when people are doing wrong to one another, the only way to make it stop is to call it out. Nehemiah realized that he had to call out those who were mistreating his fellow countrymen, and do so in direct, clear terms. He called out their practices and pointed out the horrible nature of them. He was direct and clear in his words.

All too often, we are tempted to overlook the mistreatment of some people in order to maintain peace in the overall group. Sometimes, we allow practices that are clearly wrong, simply because we lack the moral courage to stand our ground. If we are going to lead people to great places, however, we cannot allow any group to be left behind in our progress. People need to come first, and projects second.

This issue arose as the work on the wall was in progress. Nehemiah stopped everything and dealt with it, before he moved on to complete the building. He knew that if he did not take a stand for those who lacked a voice, he would build a city that no one wanted to live in. So he stopped everything and called out the wrong that was being done.

Honestly, moments like this are frustrating. Most of us try to lead in such a way that things like this don't happen. But, once in a while, the wrong person enters a position of authority or the wrong group takes over a section of the organization, and before you know it, you have a mess. As the leader, when you become aware of what's happening, you get very angry. That is not how you would have treated these people. Your anger begins with a focus on the abusers, and then it gets pointed right back at you. You stand there and realize that all of this happened under your watch, and somehow you missed it. Now you are mad at them *and* yourself. But with moral courage and a willingness to set right the wrongs that have taken place, things can improve.

Call for Repentance

"So I continued, 'What you are doing is not right. Shouldn't you walk in the fear of our God to avoid the reproach of our Gentile enemies? I and my brothers and my men are also lending the people money and grain. But let us stop charging interest! Give back to them immediately their fields, vineyards, olive groves, and houses, and also the interest you are charging them—one percent of the money, grain, new wine, and olive oil.' 'We will give it back,' they said. 'And we will not demand anything more from them. We will do as you say'" (Neh. 5:9–12).

As a leader who is showing moral courage, you must lay out clear expectations to those who have been abusive within your organization. This may mean termination, or it may mean demanding a change in practice. How far your requirements go are your call as the leader. The people that you are chastising may well be friends or trusted advisors that have gone off the rails for whatever reason. But you cannot allow your desire to maintain friendships to overpower your call from God to care for those who lack a voice. You must act, and act decisively.

Nehemiah clearly spelled out his expectations and laid the choice on the table for these nobles and officials. They had likely done nothing more than reestablish the practices of previous governors. But, under Nehemiah, those old ways were not going to cut it.

As you face—and eventually call out—wrong practices, take time to ponder the situation before stepping out to speak.

Do this not so that you can find the *nicest* way to speak, but so that you can find the *clearest* way to speak. While most of your communicative energy as a leader needs to be expended on saying things kindly and directly, in moments like this, you need to be absolutely sure that your message gets through, even if it feels a bit harsh to those on the receiving end. Now, had Nehemiah simply told these jerks off and not spelled out a clear pathway forward, he would have alienated them by embarrassing them in public, while also alienating the abused by not actually solving the problem. When calling out injustice, speak with clarity and force of moral will, while pointing the direction to repentance and healing.

Create Transparency

"Then I summoned the priests and made the nobles and officials take an oath to do what they had promised. I also shook out the folds of my robe and said, 'In this way may God shake out of their house and possessions anyone who does not keep this promise. So may such a person be shaken out and emptied!' At this the whole assembly said, 'Amen,' and praised the LORD. And the people did as they had promised" (Neh. 5:12–13).

As I have dealt with people and their failings—even at times with my own—I have had a simple rule of thumb: Private failures can be dealt with privately among the leadership core of the church, but public sins must be dealt with publicly, so that everyone knows that the matter is not being ignored, downplayed, covered up, or excused.

In Nehemiah's situation, the sin was very public, therefore the repentance moment also needed to be very public. In front of the entire city, Nehemiah called out the offending nobles and officials and required them to take an oath in front of everyone that they would never again engage in such practices. This kind of transparency builds trust in the under-empowered. Honestly, the under-empowered have heard the apologies before and seen the evil practices continue. Oh, they might stop for a while. But as soon as no one is looking, it all starts right back up again! For this reason, trust is very hard to achieve among people who have traditionally been mistreated. Public transparency and commitment to change is a great first step to renewed trust.

Commit to Be an Example

"Moreover, . . . neither I nor my brothers ate the food allotted to the governor. But the earlier governors—those preceding me—placed a heavy burden on the people and took forty shekels of silver from them in addition to food and wine. . . . I did not act like that. Instead, I devoted myself to the work on this wall. . . . Furthermore, a hundred and fifty Jews and officials ate at my table, as well as those who came to us from the surrounding nations. . . . Remember me with favor, my God, for all I have done for these people" (Neh. 5:14–19).

In the end you cannot practice moral courage while living in immorality. That is called hypocrisy. Nehemiah made a point to live out his commands to these officials at an even higher level than he expected of them. He wanted to always be certain that he was living above reproach, so that he could be the example of what was right in the face of those who would so easily give in to what was wrong. This kind of moral fortitude is what empowers moral courage and allows one to practice moral correction. Without personal commitment to deep moral norms, you cannot muster the strength or platform to demand moral reform.

PART 5

I AM THREATENED

No great work will ever go unchallenged. Anytime you are working to accomplish a calling from God, there will be threats to the progress of the project. Those threats will come in different forms and from different sources. Some of the threats will be directed at you personally, as people who want to derail you threaten you with slander, business and political reprisals, legal challenges, or even physical harm. These types of threats have, at one time or another, entered the life of any leader of any sizable organization. There is always someone who does not want you to succeed.

One of the most important things you can do for yourself when facing these threats is to try and understand where the threats are coming from. Why is this person so set against you or your organization? What hurts have they experienced, and did you intentionally or unintentionally have anything to do with those hurts? What fears do they harbor about what you are trying to do? What ambitions of theirs is your success threatening? All of these can be reasons for opposition and threats to your work and you personally. The more you understand why you are being threatened, the better you will be able to address the threats and perhaps even defuse the anger altogether.

The most difficult threats to deal with are the ones that come from people who just don't like you or your organization. Often these people cannot really explain to you why they don't like you; they just don't. Although this seems entirely irrational, it is also virtually irreversible. If someone doesn't have a good reason for not liking you or the organization you lead, then they will not be able to find a good reason to stop disliking you. In some cases like these, you will simply have to accept the animosity that is being directed your way and move on. Nehemiah faced plenty of threats as he worked to rebuild Jerusalem. How he dealt with the threats that were aimed at him can perhaps help us deal with those that are aimed at us.

23

Understand Ownership

*But when Sanballat the Horonite, Tobiah the Ammonite official
and Geshem the Arab heard about it, they mocked and ridiculed
us. "What is this you are doing?" they asked. "Are you rebelling
against the king?" I answered them by saying, "The God of
heaven will give us success. We his servants will start rebuilding,
but as for you, you have no share in Jerusalem or any claim
or historic right to it."*

—Nehemiah 2:19–20

Moral and historical claim can bring physical and emotional
strength.

So, here we are back at the beginning. The work had not yet
started, but the threats were rolling in. These three leaders—
Sanballat, Tobiah, and Geshem—were likely the leaders of the
people groups that were regularly invading Jerusalem and
entrapping her residents in a perpetual cycle of poverty. These
guys had been stealing from Jerusalem and its inhabitants for
years, and they thought it was a pretty good setup. The Jews did
the work, and they swooped in to take the profits. Nehemiah's

desire to build a wall threatened their profit margins. If they could no longer raid Jerusalem, they would lose a great revenue stream. They were not about to let that happen without at least trying to put a stop to it. So, they started with mocking: "What do you guys think you are doing?" "You can't do that!" "Who do you think you are?" When that didn't get the reaction they were looking for, they moved on to accusing: "Are you rebelling against the king?" They knew full well that Nehemiah had arrived with letters from the king, giving permission and resources for what he intended to do. But if they could cause Nehemiah or the people to doubt their safety, perhaps they might cause this effort to fall apart.

Nehemiah was having none of it. His response is a great lesson on how to respond to the irrational and untrue allegations that leaders often experience when they are making progress that others view as a threat.

Point Out Your Strength

"The God of heaven will give us success" (Neh. 2:20).

Nehemiah started by establishing that the call to rebuild the city and the strength to get it done came not from Nehemiah, the people of Jerusalem, or the faraway king who sent letters of endorsement with Nehemiah. No, the strength to get all of this done came from the God who called them to do it in the first place.

This position of strength communicated a few important details to these newfound enemies. First, if they resisted this project, they were not fighting against Nehemiah, but against God himself. This put these detractors on notice that they were dealing with a whole new type of Jew. For their entire lives, the Jews of Jerusalem had been powerless and weak. They lacked direction, vision, purpose, resources, and backing. But now they had all of that, and it was provided miraculously by their God. Just like the inhabitants of Jerusalem had grown up hearing stories of how powerful their God was when they entered the land, so had Sanballat, Tobiah, and Geshem. They knew of the powerful God of the Jews who led them to destroy all of the former inhabitants of this land. If that God was back, it might not be a good idea to fight him.

Once people realize that you view your current work as a God-given mission and calling, they tend to realize that you will not be discouraged into stopping. People who are engaged in a spiritual calling tend to see it through. Furthermore, trying to win a fight against someone who is convinced they are on a holy mission is really bad business. You leave them with an impossible choice. Give in to your demands and fail their God, or keep fighting you no matter what to please their God. They will choose their God over you almost every time.

State Clearly Your Purpose

"We his servants will start rebuilding" (Neh. 2:20).

Nehemiah left no doubt or confusion about what was about to happen. They would be taking up shovels and starting work the next day. It was as if he was saying, "Talk all you want, insult us all you want, and stand there and laugh all you want, but we are going to get to work."

When a leader clearly states purpose and next steps, people are usually comforted and strengthened by the leader's resolve. If the leader is willing to stand strong, then they can stand strong too. As Nehemiah clearly and confidently declared what was about to happen, he weakened the resolve of his enemies and strengthened the resolve of his people. He showed courage in the face of the threat and determination in answering the threat. All of this is imperative when a leader is threatened.

The other side of this truth is that leaders who get shaken when threatened and seem unconvinced of future success embolden their enemies and dishearten their followers. No one wants to follow a doubting leader into battle—especially when their city and family are at stake. The people you lead will follow with slightly less confidence than you lead with. You are the leader, and therefore, you should be the one with the greatest level of resolve. They are following you, not the other way around. So, don't lose heart just because someone called you names or made some veiled threat. If you do, your people will lose heart, and your progress will lose steam.

Establish Your Moral Ground

"But as for you, you have no share in Jerusalem or any claim or historic right to it" (Neh. 2:20).

It may seem that Nehemiah was stating the obvious, but it was very important that he do so. Remember that Jerusalem had been falling victim to attacks from neighboring cities and tribes. Likely Sanballat, Tobiah, and Geshem were responsible for some or all of those attacks. The people who had been living in Jerusalem knew these three and likely knew that they had been causing much of their distress. No one had shown the strength or backing to make them stop it. But then, Nehemiah had arrived. In his first recorded encounter with them, he laid out the new reality in no uncertain terms: "You don't belong here! There is nothing in this city that is yours! And there is nothing in the past that gives you any legal claim to anything here. So, stay out!"

I bet the residents of Jerusalem had waited their entire lives to hear somebody tell those guys that! The residents of Jerusalem, who had been cowering before these guys their entire lives, felt their backs stiffen and their chests lift. They had a leader. They had a purpose. They had a defender! And those punks were done!

That must have been a great day! Funny, isn't it, how something that started as threat, designed to discourage, became a rallying cry and encouragement? When you handle threats properly, that is exactly what can happen.

24

Ignore Name Calling

When Sanballat heard that we were rebuilding the wall, he became angry and was greatly incensed. He ridiculed the Jews, and in the presence of his associates and the army of Samaria, he said, "What are those feeble Jews doing? Will they restore their wall? Will they offer sacrifices? Will they finish in a day? Can they bring the stones back to life from those heaps of rubble—burned as they are?" Tobiah the Ammonite, who was at his side, said, "What they are building—even a fox climbing up on it would break down their wall of stones!" Hear us, our God, for we are despised. Turn their insults back on their own heads. Give them over as plunder in a land of captivity. Do not cover up their guilt or blot out their sins from your sight, for they have thrown insults in the face of the builders. So we rebuilt the wall till all of it reached half its height, for the people worked with all their heart.

—Nehemiah 4:1–6

When your enemies resort to calling you names, you can pretty much bet they are out of other options. This is a biblical example of a temper tantrum. Sanballat and Tobiah were "greatly incensed" that the work on the wall was progressing with great speed and success. They didn't want this wall to go up. They could see their easy target becoming inaccessible to them and their guaranteed profits from raiding this unprotected city vanishing. In their anger, they simply lost it. They started ridiculing the people of Jerusalem, even to the point of demeaning the work and the workers that they actually feared. They knew that once the wall was finished it would keep them out, but instead of admitting that and working toward some type of mutually agreeable relationship, they claimed that the wall would not be capable of supporting even the weight of a fox. So, their anger had now tipped over into the ridiculous.

When your enemies tip over into the ridiculous with their assessment of you and your work, it generally means they are beginning to believe you can successfully pull this off! It is actually a positive sign. But knowing that doesn't make it any less hurtful or frustrating to hear their comments. Just as their rhetoric has changed, so also your responsibility in this moment has changed.

Consider the two steps that Nehemiah took.

Be Slow to Respond

When your enemies are tipping over into the absurd, often the best response you can give is no response. If their accusations sound ludicrous to you, they most likely sound ludicrous to most anyone else. When they begin making obviously ridiculous statements, they are actually revealing to the world their own lack of ideas, wisdom, and options. So, let them do it. You don't need to protect them from their own absurdity; let them continue to be absurd. The only thing you can accomplish by engaging with them is to lower yourself to their level, and that is not helpful to your cause.

We see examples of this daily in our current culture, and it comes from some of the highest-ranking offices in the land. From world leaders, to CEOs, to media stars, to loud-mouthed billionaires, everyone seems to be on the absurdity train! They seem to believe that they win by saying something more ridiculous than their opponent did, and it becomes little more than a race to the bottom. Avoid this trap, and you will be able to stand firm and show progress, while they show themselves to be the spoiled little children they are.

Be Quick to Pray

Honestly, I could make this a main point at every juncture in this study. Nehemiah was constantly stopping to pray over the situations he was facing. This is a practice all of us would do well to emulate. When we pray a number of things happen.

Prayer keeps us focused on what is actually important. When we take our anger to God, rather than release it in cheap and degrading words, we are reminded that our goal was never to win an argument. Our goal is, always has been, and must remain the completion of our God-given calling. Getting into a shallow, meaningless shouting match with people spouting nonsense is distracting from that goal and not helpful to its completion.

Prayer allows us to vent our worst hopes in a nonviolent way. Nehemiah's prayer for Sanballat and Tobiah was not exactly life-giving. He called on God to do some pretty horrible stuff to these two. And honestly, they may have deserved all of that and then some for the trouble they had caused. But by starting with prayer, Nehemiah was able to avoid his gut reaction to go punch those guys out! Instead, he let God deal with them. No doubt, he had suggestions for how God might deal with them. But prayer allowed him to remember that vengeance was not Nehemiah's place; it belonged to God.

In the end, if we remain focused on prayer rather than allow ourselves to be dragged into the muddy waters of anger and frustration, we can actually add to the energy of our calling. The work on the wall became more intense as a result of the opposition's temper tantrum. When the people saw their leader actually leading, instead of just standing around yelling at everyone else, they learned to trust him at a deeper level yet. With a leader they knew they could count on to keep his cool in tough situations—a leader they knew they could trust—the people were able to put all of their focus on the work.

25

Guard Against Attack

But when Sanballat, Tobiah, the Arabs, the Ammonites and the people of Ashdod heard that the repairs to Jerusalem's walls had gone ahead and that the gaps were being closed, they were very angry. They all plotted together to come and fight against Jerusalem and stir up trouble against it. But we prayed to our God and posted a guard day and night to meet this threat. Meanwhile, the people in Judah said, "The strength of the laborers is giving out, and there is so much rubble that we cannot rebuild the wall." Also our enemies said, "Before they know it or see us, we will be right there among them and will kill them and put an end to the work." Then the Jews who lived near them came and told us ten times over, "Wherever you turn, they will attack us." Therefore I stationed some of the people behind the lowest points of the wall at the exposed places, posting them by families, with their swords, spears and bows. After I looked things over, I stood up and said to the nobles, the officials and the rest of the people, "Don't be afraid of them. Remember the Lord, who is great and awesome, and fight for your families, your sons and your daughters, your wives and your homes." When our enemies heard that we were aware of their plot and that God had frustrated it, we all returned to the wall, each to our own work. From that day on, half of my men did the work, while the other half were equipped with spears, shields, bows and armor. The officers posted themselves behind all the people of Judah who were building the wall. Those who carried materials did their work with one hand and held a weapon in the other, and each of the builders wore his sword at his side as he worked. But the man who sounded the trumpet stayed with me. Then I said to the nobles, the officials and the rest of the people, "The work is extensive and spread out, and we are widely separated from each other along the wall. Wherever you hear the sound of the trumpet, join us there. Our God will fight for us!" So we continued the work with half the men holding spears, from the first light of dawn till the stars came out. At that time I also said to the people, "Have every man and his helper stay inside Jerusalem at night, so they can serve us as guards by night and as workers by day." Neither I nor my brothers nor my men nor the guards with me took off our clothes; each had his weapon, even when he went for water."

—Nehemiah 4:7–23

With sufficient preparation for defense, threats tend to remain only threats.

Every leader should anticipate and watch for threats to the safety of the calling he or she is working on and the people he or she is called to lead. Threats are always present, though not always seen. Anytime progress is being made on a project that another group of people disagrees with, there will be threats. Sometimes these threats are legal, sometimes they are political, and sometimes they are physical. No matter the kind of threat, leaders must take sufficient steps to guard against it.

In Nehemiah's case, the threat was a literal, physical, military threat. The surrounding enemies had finally become so frustrated with the progress on the wall that they were preparing for a military incursion into the city to put a stop to the building. These enemies realized that once the wall was completed, and the city was defended, they would lose their place as the power brokers in the region. They understood that the Jewish people, who had been so powerless for generations, now had the potential to rise and capably defend themselves.

A people who are living in relative safety have the luxury of betterment. This is what the enemies of Jerusalem feared, and this is what the enemy of your soul fears. Once you realize that you are defended by the Holy Spirit of God, and you actually realize your identity in him, you can take your focus off of mere survival and begin building actual strength. Safety, through a well-thought-out and planned defense, gives people space to improve themselves, their communities, and the world around them. This can happen for a few key reasons.

The People Feel Cared For

When people have leaders they trust, and they see those leaders making arrangements for their safety, they feel cared for. It's not unlike a child at home. When that child is defended from any threat, real or imagined, that child feels loved and cared for. When mom or dad comes in and scares off the "monster under the bed," a child learns what it means to be defended. Where once the child felt vulnerable and threatened, now she can feel safe and defended. That's a great place to be and allows for peace deep enough to bring sleep and rest.

The People Feel Empowered

Once people see that their leadership is providing for their safety, they will join in the defense plan alongside their leaders. They will "take up arms" with their leaders and prepare themselves to fight for their families and their homes (see Neh. 4:14). This kind of shared defense responsibility builds deep strength and trust within a given community. People take responsibility for one another, and true sacrifice and service begins to occur. As a result, the community is solidified.

As the people worked in shifts to rebuild the wall and provide security for the laborers, and as they all carried swords and spears, even while working or resting at home, the people of Jerusalem began once again to see themselves as a force to be reckoned with, rather than as victims to be pitied. They no longer pitied themselves so much as they pitied the foolish band of invaders that might give it a try! It's difficult to overstate the importance of this kind of self-defense within a community. When people agree to rise up together to one another's defense, the resulting levels of commitment can become nothing short of beautiful.

The People Feel Safe

This kind of societal commitment to mutual defense of one another brings a level of safety that could never have been achieved by a hired security service or a visiting army defending Jerusalem under the orders of a faraway king. No, this kind of safety lies in knowing that your neighbor is going to show up to fight alongside you if necessary, and your neighbor knows that you will do likewise. When people feel this level of safety, they can return to their work with focus and peace. In fact, since their project was a wall that would provide an additional layer of defense, they returned to their work with added vitality. Every day, with each stone they set in place, every one of them was adding to the defense of the city. They were part of defending their brothers and sisters, sons and daughters, wives and homes. That motivation was powerful, and the work moved even faster.

This principle is played out every day in our actual lives. Even in the absence of localized physical warfare, we face spiritual, emotional, and societal threats every day. In the face of these threats to our well-being, we find peace only in knowing that we are part of a community that will "take up arms" to defend us when necessary. There, we find the safety, along with the space, to pursue betterment.

Self-improvement is not a luxury afforded to those who must spend the majority of their strength and energy just trying to survive. Only in a supportive, protective community do we find the luxury to self-improve. This is why family is so important. When our children know that we will defend them, they feel safe. When they feel safe, they find the space they need to self-improve, even self-actualize. It is in an atmosphere of defended safety that we can take the time to actually seek out, find, and settle into our proper I-am.

26

Expect Lies

When word came to Sanballat, Tobiah, Geshem the Arab and the rest of our enemies that I had rebuilt the wall and not a gap was left in it—though up to that time I had not set the doors in the gates—Sanballat and Geshem sent me this message: "Come, let us meet together in one of the villages on the plain of Ono." But they were scheming to harm me; so I sent messengers to them with this reply: "I am carrying on a great project and cannot go down. Why should the work stop while I leave it and go down to you?" Four times they sent me the same message, and each time I gave them the same answer. Then, the fifth time, Sanballat sent his aide to me with the same message, and in his hand was an unsealed letter in which was written: "It is reported among the nations—and Geshem says it is true— that you and the Jews are plotting to revolt, and therefore you are building the wall. Moreover, according to these reports you are about to become their king and have even appointed prophets to make this proclamation about you in Jerusalem: 'There is a king in Judah!' Now this report will get back to the king; so come, let us meet together." I sent him this reply: "Nothing like what you are saying is happening; you are just making it up out of your head." They were all trying to frighten us, thinking, "Their hands will get too weak for the work, and it will not be completed." But I prayed, "Now strengthen my hands."

—Nehemiah 6:1–9

Lies will be told about you, but they don't have to be validated by you.

Once Nehemiah's enemies realized they wouldn't be able to physically stop the work on the wall, they tried a new tactic, threatening to lie about him to the king. As you can imagine, if such a lie were to reach the ears of the king, and the king were to believe that Nehemiah was plotting to revolt against him from behind walls that the king himself had funded, the resulting attack would be fierce. Nehemiah's enemies had thought this through and issued the worst threat they could possibly think of. It was based on lies, but it would nevertheless be devastating should it succeed. So, they were hoping that they could get Nehemiah to come out to them, to the Valley of Ono, for a "meeting" to "negotiate" a settlement. The problem was that they planned to neither meet nor negotiate. Instead, they planned to kill Nehemiah, in hopes that his death would end the empowerment of the inhabitants of Jerusalem. Sanballat, Tobiah, and Geshem had grown weary and fearful of these Jews getting all "uppity" and not remembering their proper place. They failed to understand that it was not the Jews that had misplaced values; it was them.

Now, lies are a particularly delicate thing to defend against. In the eyes of reasonable people, most lies are easily recognized as fabrications. In our society, we have all watched as political parties lie about one another to fire up their base. The reason this works is that the base is almost never logical. To the most hardened factions in any political movement, the opposition is inherently evil. (At least that is how we are framing our political discourse these days.) When you believe the other side to be inherently evil, you will believe any lie told about them. You are not being rational. All humans are vulnerable to this, but only the most radical consistently fall victim to it. Most people can look at a lie, even about someone they politically disagree with, and see it for the falsehood that it is. When this occurs, lies have no real power. They serve only to further delude the already deluded. Therefore, in most cases, lies simply need to be allowed to suffocate from a lack of truthful oxygen.

However, there are two scenarios where lies can grow legs.

You Don't Seem Like a Good Person

Nehemiah was apparently unconcerned about the lie that was being threatened. The reason for this was his relationship with the king. The king knew and trusted Nehemiah and likely would not believe that Nehemiah would revolt against the throne. The longstanding pattern of honesty and integrity that Nehemiah had lived out before the king would protect him from the sting of these lies. However, if Nehemiah had not always been so trustworthy, the king might have had reason to pause and consider the possibility that these lies held some truth.

It is imperative, as a leader, that you maintain a reputation of integrity. That reputation will be the only thing that protects you when enemies lie about you. Think about it. When an enemy lies about you to a neighbor, no one is going to draw a sword and defend your honor; they are just going to listen. Once hearing the lie, that neighbor is going to weigh what they have heard against what they have always known about you. If they have always known you to be a person of integrity, the lie has no power. But, if they have known you to skirt around integrity, the lie, even with no shred of evidence, has power. The work of defending our leadership against lies must be done over the years that precede the lie.

Thou Doth Protest Too Much

When someone jumps too quickly or too strongly to their own defense, it causes people to wonder. The phrase I have used in the heading comes from William Shakespeare's play *Hamlet*. In the play, Prince Hamlet puts on a play (within the play) to see if he can get a reaction from those watching that would help him determine who may have murdered his father, the king. In Hamlet's play, the fictional queen goes on and on about how she would never remarry should something happen to the king. Hamlet then asks the real queen, his mother Queen Gertrude, what she thinks of the fictional character.

Her response is, "The lady doth protest too much, methinks."
Thus, Shakespeare gives voice to a natural reaction when
someone seems a little too defensive.

When we overreact to lies told about us, we give them legs.
People who would normally not be inclined to believe such
terrible things suddenly find themselves wondering why we are
so over the top in our own defense. This will give life to the lie.

So, live out your life in such a way as to defend against lies
without words, and when the lies do come, you will not need
to "protest too much, methinks."

Anticipate Espionage

One day I went to the house of Shemaiah son of Delaiah, the son of Mehetabel, who was shut in at his home. He said, "Let us meet in the house of God, inside the temple, and let us close the temple doors, because men are coming to kill you—by night they are coming to kill you." But I said, "Should a man like me run away? Or should someone like me go into the temple to save his life? I will not go!" I realized that God had not sent him, but that he had prophesied against me because Tobiah and Sanballat had hired him. He had been hired to intimidate me so that I would commit a sin by doing this, and then they would give me a bad name to discredit me. Remember Tobiah and Sanballat, my God, because of what they have done; remember also the prophet Noadiah and how she and the rest of the prophets have been trying to intimidate me.

—Nehemiah 6:10–14

Your greatest threats come from the inside.

The worst moments in every leader's life and career are those when hurt and betrayal come from inside what should be our safe space—from among those we trust. These types of hurts are particularly damaging. This is true because of the close range at which the damage is inflicted. When those who are inside of the relative safety of our walls inflict injury on us, it generally comes as a surprise or a shock. The unexpected nature of the attack compounds the hurt and deepens the wounds. While there are many reasons that someone from the inside might turn against us, let's consider a few in order to help us watch for potential flash points.

The Well-Meaning Saboteur

As a leader of any organization or project, you will often face people who do not agree with the project or the way it is progressing. At times a person who is on your team can feel that the direction you are leading is so wrong or dangerous that they will go rogue and begin to work against you, while seemingly still standing beside you. The danger is that you may not see the undercutting of your authority and leadership until it is irreversible.

Like Nehemiah, you must count on the guidance of the Holy Spirit to show you motives that you cannot otherwise see. When the prophet in this passage called for Nehemiah to close himself off in the temple, basically hiding away in fear like a coward, Nehemiah realized that the prophet was no longer speaking in the best interests of Nehemiah or Jerusalem. In fact, the prophet had been paid off by the enemies of Jerusalem and was now working for them.

Now, I realize that I am potentially giving a pass to Shemaiah by suggesting that perhaps he was, at his core, well meaning. In my experience, I have found it easier to understand these types of undermining actions if I can see them coming from a misguided heart rather than from a hostile heart. When I engage in a constant pattern of looking for hostile hearts around me, I find the roots of paranoia setting up inside of me. However, if I can assume pure motives, I will look for misguided actions while avoiding paranoid decision-making. Paranoia will not help anyone in these cases. It will actually strengthen the hand of the conspirators by making you look less than sane. So, at least for me, the possibility of a pure, yet misguided motive that causes some of these kinds of actions helps me remain both diligent and compassionate.

The Wounded Warrior

Leaders also sometimes face wounded warriors in their midst. These folks have been on the team and have been loyal, in some cases for many years. They have made sacrifices for the project, and you, as leader, have made sacrifices for them. Yet, for whatever reason, conflict has arisen between the two of you, and that conflict has ended with them feeling wounded or hurt. As a result, they can sometimes feel obligated to put you in your place or knock you down a notch or two. Folks in this category feel a "righteous" call to thwart your work. They believe that they are the ones hearing the voice of God and their spirituality demands that they take the lead and stop you from making any further progress.

These folks are often, at their core, well meaning. They have been truly hurt, and they have, rightly or wrongly, assigned responsibility for that hurt to you. This hurt, once assigned to you, puts them in a place where they feel a responsibility to protect others within the organization from being hurt by you as well. This gives their battle a very self-righteous edge and makes them exceptionally dangerous. They can declare a "holy war" before you even realize that they are hurt so deeply. In the end, once you realize what is going on, you must stop and ask yourself a few very tough questions.

1. What part of this hurt is my fault?

If we are going to remain honest in these moments—and we must remain honest—we need to accept at least partial responsibility for the hurts that have been experienced by this team member. This was somehow a conflict between the two of you, and every conflict is two-sided. You must own the fault that is yours before you move forward in any way.

2. How much damage can this person cause?

You must honestly assess what the potential fallout could be from this person's rampage. What is the worst-case scenario? Don't get caught up in paranoia. As mentioned before, that can only make the situation worse. But do take the time to consider what damage could be wrought by this person, in this position, at this time. That way you will be able to assess the actual risk your project or your organization is facing.

3. How can I mitigate that damage?

I call this "bubble wrapping" a situation. Once you have assessed your role in the hurt that has been experienced and assessed the potential damage the angry team member can inflict, you can then start the work of shielding the organization, to the greatest degree possible, from the jostling that is going to result from this team member's potential rampage. This must be done carefully and thoughtfully, but it must be done.

4. Can this person possibly continue on in a healthy way with the team?

In the end you must ask the most difficult question: Can this person remain on our team? This is always a difficult question, but in this scenario, it is made even more difficult due to the role you have played in the hurt that has brought all of this about. You must make this choice while weighing out your own emotions. Hurt people will hurt you, and angry people will anger you. You must not make this choice out of hurt and anger, but out of honest assessment of future potential. If this person can bring positive growth and movement, then work hard to work it out and keep them on board. If their anger or the actions that have already been taken preclude the possibility of a positive future, then you must remove them from the team.

The Angry Antagonist

As you lead, you will eventually run into people who, for whatever reason, are angry with choices you have made or have not made. The anger these folks express may be logical or it may be entirely irrational. The difference between this group of people and the wounded warrior type is that these folks do not have a good reason for their anger, and quite honestly, you do not have a real role in causing it. These folks often show up following a decision or choice you made that seemed entirely benign to you at the time. You changed the color scheme in the lobby of your building, or a logo, or a simple process. This change seemed to you to be a complete nonissue, and yet, for them, it was earth shattering. And it left them angry. They will then set out on a crusade to reverse the decision, if possible, but at least to make sure everyone knows how angry they are about it. If you lead a volunteer-type organization you could lose a large number of volunteers over a moment like this. Your response should be, like Nehemiah, to look for clues or divine inspiration as to what the cause of this anger is and then address it from that point. In most cases, as we see with Nehemiah, the best way forward is to simply ignore the temper tantrum and move on with little more action than prayer. You cannot fix these situations, so handing them over in prayer to the Holy Spirit is the best way forward.

The Self-Absorbed Ambitionist

When your conflict arises from this type of person, you need to remove the cancer as quickly as possible. These people do not have the overall health of the organization or the progress of the project at heart. They are simply working to increase their own control, notoriety, or power. You cannot fix this. Only God can do that. You must constantly pray that God will help you see these types early and give you the courage to deal with them quickly. Always show grace to the greatest extent possible, but never allow these types to remain in any level of leadership within your organization. Once you have determined that this is what you are dealing with, you must—watch the wording here—release them to find the place where the Holy Spirit can use their talents to their fullest capacity. In short, if you can't fix it—and you can't fix self-centeredness—then remove it.

The real art form here is seeing and properly identifying the problem. There will always be internal struggles, and there will sometimes be internal espionage. Pray constantly for supernatural insight from the Holy Spirit to deal with internal strife with compassion, grace, strength, and speed. Like cancer, this stuff will grow and eventually attach itself to vital parts of your team and work. If not dealt with properly, it can absolutely kill any type of organization.

PART 6

I AM OFF TRACK

By chapter 13 of Nehemiah, the wall is rebuilt and the city is fully restored. More Jews have relocated back to the city, and proper organization and worship has been reestablished. Then, Nehemiah did what he had intended to do all along: he went back home to Susa. The first question the king asked Nehemiah when the idea of going to restore Jerusalem was first brought to his attention was, "How long will your journey take, and when will you get back?" (Neh. 2:6). With the city safe and restored, Nehemiah headed back to the king.

But the absence of a leader often leads to a loss of focus for the organization.

Leaders can be absent in numerous ways and for a myriad of reasons. Health or family issues can take a leader away from his or her post for a time. These types of distractions are unavoidable and often beyond anyone's control. But they still leave someone else at the steering wheel of the organization or project.

Leaders who lead effectively and at a high level for an extended amount of time can face exhaustion or burnout. When this occurs, the leader may still be in the position of authority but not acting with the authority afforded the position. Therefore, while the leader is still present, their leadership is, for a time, absent.

Whatever the type and cause of the absence, there will likely be a loss of focus for the organization or project, and that loss of focus can be detrimental or even devastating. A change in leadership, for whatever reason, changes the fundamental nature of the heart of an organization. The culture established by the founding or long-term leader will continue for a time. But ultimately, the culture must change to match the personality and style of the new leader. No one can lead someone else's organization for long without causing cultural changes, albeit unintentionally.

These changes become problematic if they alter the core purpose and value of the organization, or if the former leader returns, either expectedly or unexpectedly, and reasserts their previous leadership authority. In the case of Jerusalem and Nehemiah, both of these situations took place. After Nehemiah went back to Susa, the Jews within Jerusalem were allowed to begin living in ways that were clearly not in keeping with Jewish religious norms or expectations. Then Nehemiah returned and took back the reins of leadership. What we learn from his experience is how to take an organization or group that has lost its way and guide it back to health.

28

Restore Focus

But while all this was going on, I was not in Jerusalem, for in the thirty-second year of Artaxerxes king of Babylon I had returned to the king. Some time later I asked his permission and came back to Jerusalem. Here I learned about the evil thing Eliashib had done in providing Tobiah a room in the courts of the house of God.

—Nehemiah 13:6–7

When the main thing is no longer the main thing, the thing that replaces it is a threat.

Let's take just a moment to recall something we read in chapter 2 of Nehemiah: "When Sanballat the Horonite and Tobiah the Ammonite official heard about this, they were very much disturbed that someone had come to promote the welfare of the Israelites" (Neh. 2:10). Eliashib, the priest had given space within the temple to Tobiah for the storing of some of his things. This was clearly a violation of part of the law of God for the use of the temple, which had prohibited Ammonites from entering the temple. To make matters worse, this particular Ammonite was actively working to stop the reconstruction of the city! Yet, Tobiah still had access to this space within the temple. This was clearly a violation of the law as it pertained to the use of the temple. It was also likely a return to negative practices that had preceded Nehemiah's work—practices prohibited when Nehemiah had first restored Jerusalem. It is unlikely that Nehemiah would have overlooked Tobiah's relationship with Eliashib and the things stored in the temple during his reconstruction work, especially given the adversarial relationship between Tobiah and Nehemiah. Therefore, we must assume that, upon Nehemiah's departure to the capital city, Eliashib chose to once again violate the law of God and allow this enemy of Jerusalem back into its most sacred spaces.

Why?

This is a good question. Why do people allow things that were obviously destructive in their past to reenter their lives? Why is it that we fight so hard to overcome addictions, poor habits, and failing health only to return to the patterns that caused these things? The truth here is to be found in the relationship with the violator. The NIV Study Bible has these notes on Tobiah:

Tobiah. Means "The Lord is good." He was probably a worshiper of the Lord (Yaweh), as indicated not only by his name but also by that of his son Jehohanan (6:17–18), meaning, "The Lord is gracious." Jehohanan was married to the daughter of Meshullam son of Berekiah, the leader of one of the groups repairing the wall. (3:4, 30; 6:18) Tobiah also had a close relationship with Eliashib the priest (13:4–7).[3]

So, although Tobiah was against the rebuilding of Jerusalem, he was nonetheless well-known and well-liked among many Jews.

They had an enjoyable relationship with someone that was a danger to them.

Now, doesn't that sound familiar? Organizations, churches, businesses, and individuals often have these seemingly crazy relationships with things that are obviously threatening to their long-term health and stability. This is seen most easily in the lives of individuals. We have all watched as someone struggled with and overcame an addiction, only to fall back into it at some later point. At a moment like this, we might wonder, "Why did he go back to that thing?" The answer involves the relationship that the person had with the thing. People who struggle with any type of addiction often describe their use of that thing in relationship-type terms. Alcoholics have a relationship with alcohol. Drug addicts have a relationship with drugs. Those addicted to porn have a relationship with porn. While it may not be a normal or traditional type of relationship, it is tied, like all relationships, to a set of memories, emotions, and feelings that, in a given moment, bring joy, peace, or escape from a painful reality. The relationship is not with the bottle or the image, the relationship is with the feeling those things give. It is not the chemical or the image that is being returned to, it is the feeling that is being longed for. That longing can be an overwhelmingly powerful thing.

In this case, Eliashib had a relationship with Tobiah. They were friends and likely had been for a long time. Eliashib could easily dismiss Nehemiah's refusal to accommodate Tobiah based on the adversarial role that they had to one another and the conviction that "Nehemiah just doesn't understand. He doesn't know Tobiah the way I do. I can handle this." So, Eliashib followed orders while Nehemiah was present, and then, as soon as Nehemiah left, he went right back to the relationship.

The real problem was one of focus. No one can keep two different priorities as their top priority. One of them is going to win out. Jesus himself pointed this out in the Sermon on the Mount when he said, "No one can serve two masters. Either you will hate the one and love the other, or you will be devoted to the one and despise the other. You cannot serve both God and money" (Matt. 6:24). While Jesus specifically mentioned money, any type of addiction could be substituted. In fact, any relationship you allow to inhabit as part of your spiritual center will threaten the focus on God that belongs in that spiritual center. Once something besides God takes precedence in the house of God, you run the very real risk of allowing that relationship to become the idol that replaces God altogether.

This is what was so destructive about what Eliashib was doing. While he likely viewed it as simply helping out a friend or making room for an old relationship, the reality was much deeper. We can never allow other things to take the primary place in our spiritual lives that belongs to God. Our spiritual center must remain the God of heaven, or we will run the risk of renting out space to the very enemy of our soul.

29

Restore Purity

I was greatly displeased and threw all Tobiah's household goods out of the room. I gave orders to purify the rooms, and then I put back into them the equipment of the house of God, with the grain offerings and the incense.
—Nehemiah 13:8–9

When a spiritual invader is discovered it must be ejected entirely.

Once something is discovered that is out of place, especially in your spiritual life, you must do the work of restoring the purity of the space. Distractions and distortions of truth are especially deadly in our spiritual journey as they take our focus off God and leave us looking away from the only one who will protect and grow us. They can seem very simple and common and can feel entirely unthreatening. However, by distracting our focus from God to something—anything—else, these "rented out" spaces in our hearts are one of the greatest threats to our spiritual health and progress. As such, they must be dealt with promptly and proactively.

Throw out the problem.

Simply managing sin is really not an option here. When something is discovered in your spiritual life that takes even part of your attention away from the God who should be the sole occupant of your spiritual house, it must be thrown out quickly. It is like anything else in your house—the longer you hold on to it, the harder it is to remove.

Years ago, our family decided to adopt a cat that we found in the front yard of our church. She was obviously a feral cat whose mother had either died on the highway near us or abandoned her in the yard. We brought her home and began to raise her as a domestic cat. We soon discovered that feral can be a difficult thing to work out of a cat's heart. While she had no desire to go outside of our home—making her running away a nonissue—she also did not interact well with anyone who was not a normal, consistent part of our family. She actually became a danger to visitors, and we had to lock her away in a separate room when we had company. After a few years, our youngest son, Joshua, developed a pretty severe allergy to cats. As we watched his allergies continue to get worse, I finally made the dad decision, overruling everyone else in the house that wanted Joshua to just tough it out so the cat could stay indoors. I decided that she was going to be an outdoor cat. Now, Oreo, the cat, was not part of our conversations about Joshua's allergies, nor was she in agreement with her new living arrangements. But one day, while the rest of the family was away, I decided it was time for her to relocate to her new home in our backyard. She and I spent the next four hours in a chasing, wrestling, hissing, growling, scratching, and bleeding (on my part) match, as I tried to remove this threat to my son's health and my family's social freedom from my house. It wasn't until she became so exhausted that I could throw a blanket over her without her running away that I finally relocated this cat outside. She remained there for years after that and actually became a great help, as she kept birds and animals away from our fruit trees and bushes.

Outside, she was actually a blessing, but inside she had caused strife, isolation, and sickness. This is a perfect illustration of what a seemingly simple and unthreatening relationship with a person, an object, or a habit that is misplaced can cause in your spiritual life. This cat was perfectly helpful as part of our family; she just belonged outside. Her feral nature did not allow her to function well inside. Not to mention the fact that she was making one of my children sick! She had to be removed, no matter how difficult the process of removal turned out to be.

Purify the Space

Once the intruder is removed, the space must be purified. This may take many forms. There are times when a physical purification is required. If the intruder in your life is an addiction to drugs or alcohol, there may be a time of detox or withdrawal, essentially a time of physical purification. In other instances, a spiritual purification may be necessary. I have experienced times when there was a need to bring in a team of prayer warriors and clear out a space, both a physical space that surrounded a person and a spiritual space within a person. Whatever the situation calls for, take the time to purify the space.

Most of the time the process of purification is not so dramatic. Most often, it is a matter of personal prayer, worship, and Scripture reading. It may involve changing the media that surrounds your life and fills your eyes and ears. It may involve changing the artwork on the walls of your house in order to place Scripture around you. It could involve times of meditation or changing your daily routine or established calendar. Any of these can be part of the purification process.

In the event that the intruder in your life is actually another human being who is robbing you of your relationship with your God, your spouse, your family, or whomever, you will need to purify your time by removing that person from your daily social interactions, at least for a season. Space will allow for a re-prioritization of the relationships in your life. Eventually, you may be able to reintroduce this person into your social experience, but always be careful. Relationships, like addictions, have a tendency to return with all the negative damaging effects they had before.

Fill the Void with the Godly

Once he had evicted all of Tobiah's things, Nehemiah did not leave the rooms in the temple empty. No, he filled them with "the equipment of the house of God, with the grain offerings and the incense" (Neh. 13:9). These are telling items.

The "equipment of the house of God" indicates to us that we must fill our time with serving God in whatever capacity we have been skilled or called.

The "grain offerings" tell us that we need to be fully invested in worship of our God. We need to take from even the financial parts of our lives, and show surrender and glory to God. This is a clear call toward the habit of tithing, giving the first ten percent of everything to God. When we become invested in God's work with our time and money, we tend to find that our focus remains on him.

Finally, there is the "incense." This is a matter of our worship and prayer given up to God. Just like the smoke of incense overtakes our senses and rises up to the heavens as a sweet aroma, so our worship should be allowed to overtake our senses and rise to God's presence. In this way we refill the spaces in our lives with what should have been there to begin with. While we will look further into some of these things in a moment, let me caution you here about leaving any spaces within your spiritual life empty for too long.

Once, while Jesus was speaking to the crowds, he came across a demon-possessed man. This is an obvious example of allowing something to dwell in our spiritual life that does not belong. Jesus cast out that evil spirit and then gave this warning: "When an impure spirit comes out of a person, it goes through arid places seeking rest and does not find it.

Then it says, 'I will return to the house I left.' When it arrives, it finds the house swept clean and put in order. Then it goes and takes seven other spirits more wicked than itself, and they go in and live there. And the final condition of that person is worse than the first" (Luke 11:24–26). Jesus' warning should be taken seriously. Empty spaces within our spiritual lives are open opportunities for the enemy of our souls to introduce some truly destructive, impure practices and spirits. To deny him room to work with, fill every space in your spiritual life with work, generosity, and worship of your God. When the room is already full, it tends to not get rented out!

30

Restore Generosity

I also learned that the portions assigned to the Levites had not been given to them, and that all the Levites and musicians responsible for the service had gone back to their own fields. So I rebuked the officials and asked them, "Why is the house of God neglected?" Then I called them together and stationed them at their posts. All Judah brought the tithes of grain, new wine and olive oil into the storerooms. I put Shelemiah the priest, Zadok the scribe, and a Levite named Pedaiah in charge of the storerooms and made Hanan son of Zakkur, the son of Mattaniah, their assistant, because they were considered trustworthy. They were made responsible for distributing the supplies to their fellow Levites.

—Nehemiah 13:10–13

Generosity, as a matter of worship, is central to a strong spiritual life.

One of the first signs of getting off track spiritually is a loss of generosity toward God and the church. It is an age-old truth about us human beings that we find it very difficult to worship our God by giving to him from the fruits of the labor that consumes the majority of our waking hours. When we fail to practice financial worship, the result is that people begin to wonder, "Why is the house of God neglected?" I have visited so many churches where this is the case. Somehow the congregation has stopped taking care of the church property, and the results are obvious and sad. When I go through a neighborhood and there is a church—presumably a symbol of the cleansing and uplifting power of God—that is an eyesore to the community, it just makes me a bit sick. How can we communicate the improving, healing power of God, when our property needs improvement and repair? Why would a community trust us to care for their eternal soul when we cannot even care for our front yard? This type of failure must be dealt with at the very core of the problem. We must begin to understand that our financial worship is a major part of our overall worship and is the most visible part of our witness to our surrounding community.

Lack of Personal Generosity Produces a Lack of Corporate Worship

"All the Levites and musicians responsible for the service had gone back to their own fields" (Neh. 13:10).

Those who work in the church, or work at the arts of the church, must take care of their homes, families, spouses, and children, just like everyone else. Therefore, they have to get paid, or they have to find other work. Here we have a key example of what happens when the people of God neglect the generosity that is required of them by God. Again, this generosity of spirit is part of our worship. It is no fundraising ploy to remind God's people of the tithe that has been required and expected from God's people throughout the existence of the nation of Israel all the way through till today. The result of losing this surrender to generosity is obvious to everyone. When a congregation loses its focus on generosity, then the work of the church suffers, and at times, ceases.

It is a real part of life that everything costs money. It requires money to run anything. But somehow people expect the church to have no concern for money. When a pastor reminds the people of the biblical mandate to tithe and give offerings, that pastor is often berated as greedy or only interested in money. I find it interesting that we don't fault anyone else in society for their efforts, even demands, to raise money. Frankly, government raises money at the point of a gun and is celebrated for all it does. Corporations set prices in a clear effort to enrich those at the top at the highest levels, and they are celebrated for all they do. Yet, somehow, when the church raises money the way the Bible tells us to, we are berated. What gives? The people of God must remain surrendered to the call of God to give. Only then can the blessing of God and the redemption of God be spread abroad to all those who have not yet heard.

Lack of Corporate Integrity Can Produce a Lack of Personal Generosity

"I put Shelemiah the priest, Zadok the scribe, and a Levite named Pedaiah in charge of the storerooms and made Hanan son of Zakkur, the son of Mattaniah, their assistant, because they were considered trustworthy" (Neh. 13:13).

We do have to admit that, at times, some who lead churches have been less than honorable with how the money is handled. When this occurs, in any congregation, it hurts the entire church. The community surrounding the church hears of the mismanagement of funds, and they begin to question or lose faith in their own congregation or church leaders. It is imperative that the church be financially managed with the highest levels of integrity and transparency. While everyone does not have to see everything, there must be an acceptable level of accessibility to the congregation to ensure trust in the honesty and integrity of the leadership. We have all seen examples of pastors who have mismanaged funds, treasurers who have embezzled funds, and boards of directors that have misused funds. These are never acceptable practices and bring great harm to the overall health of the church at large. Therefore, the church must find leaders who are "considered trustworthy" to manage the financial health of any congregation. While it is the responsibility of the individual worshiper to bring the tithe into God's house, it is the responsibility of the leaders of the church to properly manage the tithes brought in.

Corporate Integrity Plus Personal Generosity Restores Spiritual Focus

 "They were made responsible for distributing the supplies to their fellow Levites" (Neh. 13:13).

When the leadership of the church takes proper care of those who work in the church, the work of the gospel is allowed to continue with power and focus. It is the responsibility of the leadership structure of the church—be that a board of administration, a board of elders, or an oversight board made up of leaders from other places—to ensure that the workers are properly compensated for their work. The apostle Paul commanded this when he wrote to Timothy and said, "The elders who direct the affairs of the church well are worthy of double honor, especially those whose work is preaching and teaching. For Scripture says, 'Do not muzzle an ox while it is treading out the grain,' and 'The worker deserves his wages'" (1 Tim. 5:17–18). This clearly shows that those who work faithfully and effectively in the church deserve to be compensated. It is the responsibility of the church leadership structure to see to it that the compensation given to their workers is fair and reasonable. No board should view it as their responsibility to over-compensate church workers, nor should they see it as their responsibility to "keep them humble" by keeping them poor. There are plenty of groups out there who will help leadership boards know what is appropriate compensation based on level of responsibility, area of the country in which the congregations exists, and size of attendance, budget, or staff. All of these factors must be taken into account fairly. Once this is taken care of, then the workers in the church can focus on the ministry of the church and the gospel of Christ can be spread to those around the church.

31

Restore Balance

In those days I saw people in Judah treading winepresses on the Sabbath and bringing in grain and loading it on donkeys, together with wine, grapes, figs and all other kinds of loads. And they were bringing all this into Jerusalem on the Sabbath. Therefore I warned them against selling food on that day. People from Tyre who lived in Jerusalem were bringing in fish and all kinds of merchandise and selling them in Jerusalem on the Sabbath to the people of Judah. I rebuked the nobles of Judah and said to them, "What is this wicked thing you are doing—desecrating the Sabbath day? Didn't your ancestors do the same things, so that our God brought all this calamity on us and on this city? Now you are stirring up more wrath against Israel by desecrating the Sabbath." When evening shadows fell on the gates of Jerusalem before the Sabbath, I ordered the doors to be shut and not opened until the Sabbath was over. I stationed some of my own men at the gates so that no load could be brought in on the Sabbath day. Once or twice the merchants and sellers of all kinds of goods spent the night outside Jerusalem. But I warned them and said, "Why do you spend the night by the wall? If you do this again, I will arrest you." From that time on they no longer came on the Sabbath. Then I commanded the Levites to purify

themselves and go and guard the gates in order to keep the
Sabbath day holy.

—Nehemiah 13:15–22

Balancing Work, Rest, and Worship Will Improve Our Health and Productivity

From the very creation of the world, God has demanded a work, worship, and rest balance among his people. This is still true today. What we observe in this passage is an Old Testament way of preserving the practice of setting aside a day for rest and worship. This day is referred to as a Sabbath day. The literal meaning is a seventh day. The idea comes from the very dawn of creation. "Thus the heavens and the earth were completed in all their vast array. By the seventh day God had finished the work he had been doing; so on the seventh day he rested from all his work. Then God blessed the seventh day and made it holy, because on it he rested from all the work of creating that he had done" (Gen. 2:1–3).

God worked for six days to create the universe in which we live, and then God took a day off. Now, it is clear that God was not tired and in need of a vacation after six days of work. Instead, God was establishing for us a livable pattern of work, rest, and worship. Today we are aware, from multiple studies of humans and work patterns, that properly managed time off from work actually increases health and productivity among workers. It seems counterintuitive to think that productivity will increase with fewer working hours, but it does. It is easier to understand that some time off will increase the mental and physical health of individuals. All of this is simply what God told us was true about humanity from the beginning, and now science has studied it and decided they agree with God.

These days we don't live in a culture that sets laws closing everything down on a given day of the week. Instead, we must take authority in our own lives to create the necessary space for rest and worship. Honestly, most people work and most people work hard. The issue most often is not about getting people to work. The issue is getting them to properly rest from work and using part of that rest time to worship the God who has given them the ability and opportunity to work in the first place. While Nehemiah's approach of enforcing through penalty of law a work-rest-worship pattern in life was normal for his day, we cannot, and should not, attempt such government-sponsored spirituality today. Our spiritual and physical health is our personal responsibility.

Sometimes we can seem entirely unconcerned about either. You must find time for rest. If you don't, you will burn out and eventually be unhelpful to anyone. It is during times of exhaustion and burnout that I most often see pastors and church leaders fail in their work life and in their moral lives. Lack of rest can leave you unable to properly see or process the world around you. Things that you would normally never consider doing somehow seem acceptable when viewed through an exhausted mind. Likewise, when people allow themselves to become spiritually depleted, their view of the world around them is skewed in unhealthy ways. Your discipline of rest and worship will strengthen you, if you will make it a priority in your life. If you do not, your lack of discipline will undo you.

32

Restore Worship

So I purified the priests and the Levites of everything foreign, and assigned them duties, each to his own task.
—Nehemiah 13:30

Worship keeps life centered on what really matters.

We will spend the entirety of the next part of this book focused on worship. Let it suffice to say here that at the end of Nehemiah's reforms—both times—he closed out his work with worship. I believe this to be a core understanding of the power of worship in the life of a believer. When we take time to worship our God, we get our minds and spirits focused on the very Creator, Sustainer, Savior, and Center of all things.

Our God made us, and he made us to worship him. When we keep that worship as a central focus and a core discipline of our lives, we are able to see and understand the rest of the world from a Spirit-led perspective and interact with those around us from a Spirit-empowered place. This will allow us to have more than just an impact on the people we love and live around the most. This will allow our impact on them to be of an eternal, spiritual nature. This is what we bring to the table: the eternal hope of spiritual balance found in an everlasting God. When we lose sight of him, I am afraid we no longer have anything of value to offer.

PART 7

I AM GOD'S

*I saw, that, "simplicity of intention, and purity of affection,"
one design in all we speak or do, and one desire ruling all our
tempers, are indeed "the wings of the soul," without which
she can never ascend to the mount of God.*[4]

—John Wesley

I love this quote from John Wesley. I realize that his English
was a little old school, but what he said still strikes to the
center of what you and I need to be reaching toward. Wesley
wrote these words in the opening pages of his *Plain Account
of Christian Perfection*. He was describing how he came to
understand the holiness doctrine that would become his
crowning teaching and achievement. But instead of getting
involved with Wesley's theology, get lost for a moment in those
words. He was advocating a "simplicity of intention," a "purity of
affection," and a singular desire that will rule "all our tempers."

This singularity of purpose and thinking would, Wesley believed, give our faith "the wings of the soul," without which "she can never ascend to the mount of God." The words here are beautiful, and I hope they truly spark something within your soul.

What Wesley sparks, at least for me, is that reality that lingers just beneath the surface of our mundane daily lives. It is the knowledge that there is more there than I now see. That knowledge drives me to a single-minded pursuit of the God who created me, sacrificed for me, died for me, forgave me, indwells me, and guides me on a daily basis. This life-long and all-consuming pursuit of God is, in my estimation, worship. It is the realization that I am a servant of God, and more than that, I am a child of God. I should honestly desire that my life be lived out in a single-minded pursuit of the God who knows all, sees all, comprehends all, and is all. When we short-circuit this relationship, we miss the most important thing of all thing—the realization that I am God's! This reality is the ultimate shaper of my true, eternal identity.

So many have missed this profound truth to their own peril. When we devote our lives to the pursuit of lesser things, we attain lesser things. When we devote our lives to fully knowing the God of heaven to the deepest, highest, widest, and most surrendered levels of relationship, we attain the greatest of all knowing and the freest of all being. This pursuit of God is what will characterize this final chapter. The ultimate goal is the ability and capacity to freely, effectively, and simply pursue a relationship with the God who has called us his own.

Read His Word

So on the first day of the seventh month Ezra the priest brought the Law before the assembly, which was made up of men and women and all who were able to understand. He read it aloud from daybreak till noon as he faced the square before the Water Gate in the presence of the men, women and others who could understand. And all the people listened attentively to the Book of the Law.

—Nehemiah 8:2–3

Reading God's Word brings understanding of God's Truth. The rebuilding of Jerusalem was complete by the end of chapter 6, and in chapter 7 we see Nehemiah taking a census of everyone who was then in the city. Having rebuilt the city and reestablished the population, Nehemiah turned the attention of the entire city toward the God for whom the city was built in the first place. His first act after securing the city and returning the population was to "bring out the Book of the Law of Moses" (Neh. 8:1). Nehemiah had the Book of the Law read aloud in the presence of "all who were able to understand" (v. 2). He wanted these renewed citizens of a rebuilt city to truly understand what all of this was about. He wanted them to know their God.

Our understanding of the God we serve is to be found in his revelation of himself to us through his Word, the Bible. While it is true that we can experience God the Holy Spirit in very real spiritual ways on a daily basis without reading the Bible, we cannot understand what we experience of the Holy Spirit without filtering it through the Bible. Our Bibles are our lens through which to see the God that we serve and that we have come to love. In his Word, God reveals himself to us in ways that give clarity to our experiences with the Holy Spirit. The apostle Peter tells us that we "have been born again, not of perishable seed, but of imperishable, through the living and enduring word of God. For, 'All people are like grass, and all their glory is like the flowers of the field; the grass withers and the flowers fall, but the word of the Lord endures forever.' And this is the word that was preached to you" (1 Pet. 1:23–25). So, while the opinions of learned people will, and do, change like the shifting of the wind, God's Word stands forever! It is the Bible that gives meaning to all that I hear and experience of the Spirit of God.

So, why don't we read it?

Most people do not read the Bible as much as they should, and many people don't read it at all. Let's take a look at three of the most common reasons for not reading the Bible and see if we can move you past these well-used excuses.

I Don't Have Time

If we are honest with ourselves, we have to admit that we make time to do the things we really want to get done. The art of carving out time to accomplish meaningful things in our lives is called discipline. Each of us must exercise the discipline to accomplish those things that we deem important, even when we do not deem them fun or exciting. Oftentimes, the promise of fun and excitement will spark the planning and scheduling needed to accomplish a given goal. We rarely miss our vacations once we have paid even the initial down payment. No, instead we work extra hours here and there in order to exercise the discipline necessary to get to the beach, the mountains, or wherever it is that we plan to go next.

Why is discipline easier in these matters than with other things like Bible reading? Simple: it's more fun.

I'm not going to try and suggest to you that reading your Bible—or reading anything, for that matter—is always fun and exciting. I understand that most people just don't view it that way. But it is worthwhile to everyone and simply imperative to those who want to effectively become more like Christ. The discipline necessary to ensure Bible reading is far more akin to the discipline required to work out or get to the gym on a regular basis. While you realize that the next hour or so of your life may not be the most fun you will have all day, you know that it will make you better, and in the end, will pay dividends that are worthwhile. Like your diet, exercise, education, and work schedule, Bible reading sometimes falls into that category of things I must do, even though there might be other things I prefer to do.

Which brings me to my ultimate point. When you say you don't have time to read the Bible, well, that just isn't true. Now, hold on, I'm not suggesting you are lying; I am suggesting that you are deceived. You see, as you go through your day and rush from one thing to another, you convince yourself that there just isn't time for one more thing, no matter how important, anywhere in your schedule. But, if the motivation was great enough, you would make room for that one more thing. You might have to move some work hours, if that is possible for you; plan to multitask, while the kids are at soccer practice; skip a less-important meeting or group; get up earlier; or stay up later. Somehow, if the motivation is great enough, you will work it out.

So, let me suggest that reading your Bible is worthy of that kind of motivation. As God's Word enters your heart and mind, it changes you for the better. It enters your thinking like a living thing that brings protection and hope. The writer of Hebrews put it this way: "For the word of God is alive and active. Sharper than any double-edged sword, it penetrates even to dividing soul and spirit, joints and marrow; it judges the thoughts and attitudes of the heart" (Heb. 4:12). That is the kind of spiritual ultrasound we need from time to time to ensure that there are no cancerous attitudes or thoughts that are invading our lives. The Bible is worthy of our time. So let me implore you to take time—to make time—to spend in the Word.

I Don't Understand

Now, here we have a little more truth involved. Most people struggle with understanding the Bible when they first start reading. This causes many to believe that, until they go and get the education they need from some college or seminary, they just won't be able to understand the Bible, and they might think, *Since I can't understand it, why read it?*

The answer is that you should read it so that you can begin to understand it.

Recently, there has been a lot of interest in the release of several superhero-type movies. These movies have come out in a given sequence, inspired by the comic books that initially inspired the characters. My wife and I have seen a couple of these movies, but honestly, not that many of them. So we went to see one called *Marvel: Infinity War*. I left the theater more than a little perturbed. It seems that this movie was a set-up for the next movie called *Marvel: Endgame*. But, here's the problem. In order to fully understand what had happened in *Infinity War*, much of which did not make sense to me, and ultimately, to understand what would happen in *Endgame*, which I was now forced to wait to see, I needed to understand and watch a bunch of other movies! I didn't understand, so I needed to watch more so that I could understand. I did not simply say, "I don't understand, so I won't watch." No, I spent some time talking to my sons, who know this stuff every bit as well as I know biblical theology. I watched some key movies, and then I went to see, and enjoyed, *Endgame*. As much as it pains me to say this, understanding the Bible works the same way as understanding the Marvel Cinematic Universe. Exposure to the material builds familiarity with the material, which in turns leads to understanding.

So, let me say it again: Read the Bible so that you can understand the Bible!

I Don't Believe

Now we are getting down to the real base of many people's hesitancy to read the Bible. While most people will agree that the Bible is a great book and should be read, most people are also not sure they believe everything in it and, therefore, are not certain they want to read it. If I may be rather blunt here, reading only what you already know you fully agree with is an ineffective way to learn and grow as a human being. We must pursue truth and knowledge, even in places that don't agree with us. As I sit in my office, with my bookshelf behind me, I could turn around and name several books on my shelf that teach "truths" that I don't believe. On my shelf I have *The Communist Manifesto* by Karl Marx. I can hardly think of a book that I disagree with more profoundly or that I think has wrought more evil on the planet than that one. But I have read it. I have on my shelf books like *God Is Not Great* by Christopher Hitchens and *The Koran* by Muhammad. I don't agree with the "truth" these authors write, but that does not mean I should not expose myself to that "truth." Honestly, most of the books on my shelf have something in them that

I don't agree with. But all of them have given me insight into something that God ultimately used to help me grow as a human. If for no other reason, you should read your Bible to expose yourself to a set of truths that have arguably had a greater impact on mankind than any other written word.

34

Celebrate His Presence

*Ezra opened the book. All the people could see him because he was standing above them; and as he opened it, the people all stood up. Ezra praised the L*ORD*, the great God; and all the people lifted their hands and responded, "Amen! Amen!" Then they bowed down and worshiped the L*ORD* with their faces to the ground.*

—Nehemiah 8:5–6

When God shows up, we bow down.

I love the image we see in this account. Ezra, the scribe, brings out the Book of the Law, and as he prepares to read it in the presence of all the people, they all stand in reverence for the Word of God. These people are gathered for the dedication of their newly rebuilt city. Ezra was brought back to Jerusalem under an order given by Cyrus, king of Persia, and his main focus was the rebuilding of the temple under the guidance of Zerubbabel, the governor over the province and thought to be the grandson of the last king of Judah. Now that the temple had been reconstructed, giving the people a place to worship, and the walls of the city had been rebuilt, giving the people the security and freedom to worship, they were ready to get this worship time started! So, the people built a platform for Ezra to stand on, and when he stepped up onto that platform, holding the Book of the Law, the people showed respect, praise, and honor to the God of Israel, who had brought all of this rebuilding about.

Respect

"The people all stood up" (Neh. 8:5).

Sometimes I worry about our modern culture. I worry that we have lost our sense of respect for people, offices, and institutions that have been at the center of our culture for two centuries now. I really don't want to sound like a grumpy old man, and I must admit to my role in the problem I now write about. When I was growing up, you got dressed up in your "Sunday best" to go to church. You would not think of going to church without being properly dressed. Well, that whole idea is out the window at New Life Church. I wear jeans every Sunday, and I'm the pastor! So, as you can see, I own some of the blame for this loosening of respectful norms. But often it goes deeper than wearing the right clothes. When Ezra walked out onto the platform with the Book of the Law in his hands, the people instinctively knew to stand up. They wanted to show proper respect for God's laws and decrees. They wanted to show proper respect for God. They did this by standing in his presence. In viewing the Book of the Law as representing the very presence of God, they viewed this as a moment that called for honor, respect, and dignity. So they stood.

Whenever we enter into the presence of God, we should be equally as careful to show the respect that is called for in the presence of the King of Kings. I am not suggesting that certain attire is required or that a given way of showing respect is preferable over other ways of showing respect. But I am saying that, whatever respect for the presence of God means for you, when you enter worship, practice that, and show some respect to the God who made you, saved you, dwells within you, and will one day carry you home to be with him in heaven.

Praise

"Ezra praised the Lord, the great God; and all the people lifted their hands and responded, 'Amen! Amen!'" (Neh. 8:6).

Now, I have to admit that I am a singer. Therefore, praise, to me, involves making some noise! In this account, given to us in chapters 8 through 10, Nehemiah brought out multiple choirs so that music and singing would be part of the celebration. In this verse, when Ezra praised the God of heaven, the people responded not with song, but with some hearty "Amens!" Let me confess again. Not only am I a singer, I am a preacher. Therefore, I love it when people begin with their chorus of amens during a sermon. It just gives such a burst of energy to have people agree with you in the midst of a sermon. Once the "amen crowd" starts, the preacher in me can get on a roll.

I truly do think that deeply emotional and moving worship should elicit a verbal response. There have been plenty of times when I have listened to a sermon and I just could not hold back the verbal responses. I sometimes find myself responding before I even know it. I actually think these outbursts can be part of showing respect to the God we have gathered to worship. The word *amen* itself is a term of agreement, meaning "So be it," or "It is so!"[5] Therefore, to say amen during a sermon is to shout out at the preacher, "I agree with you! You are right!" This kind of agreement with the word being preached can inspire the preacher forward and inspire those around you to agree as they hear the truth of God being proclaimed. Our praise to God can absolutely do more than just rise to heaven; it can also raise the awareness and willingness of those around us to surrender to the One who is above us all.

Honor

"Then they bowed down and worshiped the LORD with their faces to the ground" (Neh. 8:6).

After a lifetime of looking into Scripture and looking at the lives of biblical characters, I have come to believe that the most common physical position humans take when they encounter the divine is lying flat with one's face to the ground. It may seem odd that people react this way, but not after spending a great deal of time seeking the presence of the Lord. There have been multiple times in my life where I have been seeking God's presence, and the Holy Spirit just decided to move in around me with great power and let me know that he was there. In those moments, my reaction is always the same. I get down on the floor. It usually starts with me simply going to my knees, but it always ends with me flat out with my face to the floor. Often, I lie there and almost wish that I could sink into the floor, because in the presence of the Holy Spirit, I am still too elevated. His presence is overwhelming.

I wonder, sometimes, how long it will take in eternity for us to just get up off the floor when we actually see him face to face. Please don't misunderstand, this physical position is not taken out of fear. Yes, our God is a fearful and all-powerful God, but his love is just as overwhelming as his power. This is no "face on the floor because I fear God will kill me" posture. This is face on the floor because I can't think of any better way to show reverence and honor to the God who is always more and always deserves more honor than I can give!

I think this is what was going on in Jerusalem as Ezra brought out the Book of the Law. As the Israelites saw the scribe carrying this most holy of texts, and they realized that they were about to hear the Word of the Lord, they took the only position that seemed appropriate. They got themselves as low to the ground as possible, and there they stayed, until the loving voice of the Father reached out and permitted them to stand in his presence. It is here, after finding permission to stand in the presence of a God before whom you only know to bow, that the deepest and richest forms of worship happen. In my experience, there is often no music, at least not that I am paying attention to, and often there is no one else around. All of the trappings of modern worship, as wonderful and important as they may be, are torn down, and I am left with nothing more than the presence of the God who loves me enough to allow me to stand in his presence. I still feel unworthy. I still feel as though I want to sink into the concrete to perhaps get low enough to show the honor he deserves. But I am invited to stand—and know—my Lord and my God.

35

Receive His Forgiveness

On the twenty-fourth day of the same month, the Israelites gathered together, fasting and wearing sackcloth and putting dust on their heads. Those of Israelite descent had separated themselves from all foreigners. They stood in their places and confessed their sins and the sins of their ancestors. They stood where they were and read from the Book of the Law of the LORD their God for a quarter of the day, and spent another quarter in confession and in worshiping the LORD their God.
—Nehemiah 9:1–3

Confession is required in the presence of a holy God.

I remember speaking to a youth pastor once when I was a teen, as he attempted to describe our need to confess before God. As he began to talk about how we might feel in the presence of a holy God, he pointed out that when we are presented with a true image of holiness, our sinfulness becomes clearly visible. It's kind of like that tissue test that the teeth-whitening-toothpaste people want you to perform. Your teeth look plenty white and clean to you, until you put a piece of clean white tissue paper up against them. Then suddenly, you want to go brush your teeth again! In fact, you end up wanting to go buy their product because your teeth look so yellow. What once was all good suddenly seems almost embarrassing. Most of us have had this experience.

The problem with the teeth-versus-tissue-paper example is a very close comparison to the me-versus-a-holy-God example. We are comparing two things that are just not comparable. In the teeth-versus-tissue-paper example, we must remember that no one is born with teeth that white. These companies are only attempting to establish an impossible norm in order to sell an unnecessary product. With the me-versus-a-holy-God example, the first truth remains the same. No one is born that holy! However, in a given moment, when God allows us, through his presence or his Word, to see him in all his holiness and capture just a glimpse of what he is like, he is not attempting to sell us some product, nor is he attempting to leave us discouraged and hopeless due to our own sin. No, God is showing us the purity that is possible and will one day be a reality for us as we follow him in this life and ultimately end up in front of him in heaven. God is allowing us to see a target that is always beyond our reach but still worth pursuing, because the closer we get the better we are.

However, by allowing us to catch a glimpse of his holiness, God inevitably reveals to us our sinfulness. The dingy, stained reality of who we actually are is fully revealed when held up to the perfect unblemished reality of who God is. This experience is sobering, to say the least, but it is also motivating. Our God does not show us himself and teach us to follow him in an attempt to depress us. No, God shows us himself in an attempt to draw us into an ever-deepening and ever-purifying relationship with him. This relationship will renew us, change us, and make us holy like he is holy, if we will surrender to it.

The first step in that surrender is confession.

Let's be honest. It is not like it isn't obvious that we have much to confess! Especially the first time we encounter a holy God or his holy Word. Our confession is a simple acceptance of reality. God is holy and we are not . . . yet. But he offers us a relationship that will one day draw us into the holiness now so visibly lacking as we stand next to him. I actually love the way the apostle Paul put it—the same apostle who, before surrendering to Christ, persecuted the church and found himself facedown in the dirt looking into the holiness of Christ himself. In that moment, the comparison must have been terrifyingly vivid for the apostle then known as Saul. His sin held up next to the One who had died and risen to forgive all sin. His hatred of all things non-Jewish held up against the all-encompassing love for all mankind that vividly streamed through the very presence of the Savior, Jesus. After that moment, that realization, that confession, the apostle gives us hope. "If you declare with your mouth, 'Jesus is Lord,' and believe in your heart that God has raised him from the dead, you will be saved. For it is with your heart that you believe and are justified, and it is with your mouth that you profess your faith and are saved.

As the Scripture says, 'Anyone who believes in him will never be put to shame'" (Rom. 10:9–11).

36

Establish His Ways

"In view of all this, we are making a binding agreement, putting it in writing, and our leaders, our Levites and our priests are affixing their seals to it. . . . The rest of the people—priests, Levites, gatekeepers, musicians, temple servants and all who separated themselves from the neighboring peoples for the sake of the Law of God, together with their wives and all their sons and daughters who are able to understand—all these now join their fellow Israelites the nobles, and bind themselves with a curse and an oath to follow the Law of God given through Moses the servant of God and to obey carefully all the commands, regulations and decrees of the Lord our Lord."

— Nehemiah 9:38, 10:28–29

True worship results in real change.

One of the great frustrations for pastors and church leaders is the feeling among church people that worship is an event that is limited to an hour or so on a given day of the week. In truth, we worship God with our lives—our entire lives. So, to truly worship is to truly be changed. Listen again to what the apostle

Paul had to say on this subject: "Therefore, I urge you, brothers and sisters, in view of God's mercy, to offer your bodies as a living sacrifice, holy and pleasing to God—this is your true and proper worship" (Rom. 12:1).

Your spiritual act of worship is the physical and mental work of controlling and purifying what you choose to do. That would be a revolutionary idea for most people. Most people in our culture view worship as a once-weekly event that happens at a given place called church and at a given hour. During this event, they sing, give money, and hear a message based on the Bible. If people make any decisions for change at these events, they are generally knee-jerk decisions made in an emotional moment and not shared with very many others. To be entirely honest, this approach works poorly in bringing about life change for Christ-followers.

In this account with Nehemiah and the people of Jerusalem, they took an entirely different approach to changing the lives and practices of all those who lived in Jerusalem at that time. If we used a similar process, we might see better results.

Make It Public

"On the twenty-fourth day of the same month, the Israelites gathered together, fasting and wearing sackcloth and putting dust on their heads" (Neh. 9:1).

This entire conversation concerning how the inhabitants of Jerusalem were to live in the sight of—and in the city of—their God took place in public. They truly had this conversation as a group. There was a corporate understanding that following

God was the best way forward and a further understanding that they were not properly following God. So, together, they came to a rational, considered agreement that something needed to change. The truth is that most decisions made in an emotional moment don't last. When an emotional choice is made, it is dependent on the emotion for its strength and lasting power. Once that emotional pull has lost its grip, the decision has no weight to it and quickly falls to the side. However, when time has been given to actually consider the problem and the possibilities, and when that time has been vetted through the eyes and minds of others around us who are in it with us, decisions and choices become more than emotional shifts. Real change can happen at this point because there is a rational, considered understanding of what is broken and what is best going forward.

Set Expectations

"Follow the Law of God given through Moses the servant of God and . . . obey carefully all the commands, regulations and decrees of the LORD our Lord" (Neh. 10:29).

Low expectations are a death sentence to high achievement. While it is true that sometimes people set their expectations so high that they actually set themselves up for failure, a more common problem is setting expectations so low that achievement does not bring change. This generally happens with vague and unmeasurable statements of expectation. Statements like, "I'm going to lose some weight" or "I'm going to be a better person" are just not measurable or even really meaningful. In our spiritual life, we make statements about being a "better disciple" or a "deeper Christian" or "more spiritual" and then wonder why we don't make progress. Our goals sound great, but our progress is terribly lacking.

The failure is not in the stated goal. Everyone would agree that losing weight, or being a better person, or a better disciple, or a deeper Christian, or even a more spiritual person is a good thing. But how do you plan to achieve that goal? The progress is all wrapped up in the how, and the how is completely tied to the what, or the expectations. Once you have established a fairly clear and measurable set of goals, you can easily determine how you will achieve those goals. The residents of Jerusalem set a very clear and measurable goal for themselves. They took "an oath to follow the Law of God given through Moses the servant of God and to obey carefully all the commands, regulations and decrees of the Lord our Lord" (v. 29). This was a clear, measurable goal. Now that they knew the target, the path forward became very clear. They had to do things like clean out storage rooms in the temple that had been given over to non-sacred use. They had to reschedule the weekly flea market so that it would not occur on the Sabbath. They had to return to a proper diet that was clearly spelled out for them in the law of Moses. Once they set clear, reasoned, and measurable goals, change became achievable.

Accept Accountability

"In view of all this, we are making a binding agreement, putting it in writing, and our leaders, our Levites and our priests are affixing their seals to it" (Neh. 9:38).

They wrapped it all up by making a binding agreement. Now, today we do not pass laws enforcing particular religious practices, and thank God we don't! However, our spiritual progress will not occur without accountability to someone. If control of our physical, emotional, and spiritual lives is the ultimate form of worship, then we absolutely need someone—or a group of someones—around us who will hold us accountable for our progress and our failures.

That accountability does not have to be harsh or enforced by some officer of the law with a gun and the ability to imprison. Most people truly do not want to disappoint those who are journeying with them on a given path of growth. So, the fear of disappointing others can be just as motivating as the fear of a person with a badge. This is why so many people accomplish great things in groups. Exercise groups, AA groups, weight loss groups, marriage groups—all of these use the power of community accountability to drive forward positive change.

The same principles can and should be applied in our spiritual lives. Everyone who is on a journey of spiritual growth should be surrounded by others who are also on a similar journey. In doing this we can create positive levels of community and accountability. This accountability will take our desire to change and empower it to become an effective process of change that ultimately leads to very real and lasting change. These publicly stated, clearly measured, and fully accountable goals will allow the change in our lives that is "your true and proper worship" (see Rom. 12:1).

37

Remember His Blessings

And on that day they offered great sacrifices, rejoicing because God had given them great joy. The women and children also rejoiced. The sound of rejoicing in Jerusalem could be heard far away.

—Nehemiah 12:43

God's blessings must always be remembered, communicated, and celebrated.

All too often we forget the great things that God has done for us. God's kindness to us extends from the simple provision of skills and opportunities to sustain ourselves all the way to his protective hand guarding us from disaster we never even knew was a threat. His blessings on us are never ending and quite honestly immeasurable. But they can be forgotten. In difficult times, past blessings seem to tarnish beneath the weight of our current hardship. While we may know in our minds that God has been faithful in the past, in our current moment we simply aren't sure that he will do it again. This lack of faith that God will come through for us once again can lead to a very real insecurity and can leave us feeling defeated. Our identity can return to one of brokenness, even after this entire journey to a better place, if we allow ourselves to doubt God's continued love and concern for us.

However, there is a simple solution—praise.

When we praise God for his past blessings, we remind ourselves of our future hope. Throughout history, humans have used different methods to remind themselves of the hope they have in God.

Songs

Songs have, since the dawn of time, brought great peace, hope, and strength to those who would sing them. In biblical history they harken back to the powerful goodness of God and foreshadow what that powerful God could potentially do now. These songs bring strength by reminding people where their hope has always come from. I am certain that the Israelites loved to sing the psalms of David as a reminder of how good God had always been to them. The Israelites were not the only ones to use this tactic. To this day, societies write songs about their heroes and their victories. These songs recall a time when greatness arose through a person or group and somehow saved a nation or a tribe. When these songs are sung, they can bring an entire stadium, even a nation, to their feet in pride. Here in the US, we sing our national anthem at the start of most sporting events. "The Star-Spangled Banner" is a perfect example of just such a victorious song. As Francis Scott Key wrote the lyrics to the song, he was watching from the deck of a British ship as Fort McHenry in Baltimore, Maryland, was being shelled by the cannons of this and other ships in the harbor during the dark days of the War of 1812. As he wrote, he was straining for first light of day to see if perhaps the flag of the nation he loved and called home was still flying. If you are a citizen of the US, it's going to be awfully hard for you not to sing as you read these words:

Oh, say can you see by the dawn's early light
What so proudly we hailed at the twilight's last
    gleaming?
Whose broad stripes and bright stars through the
    perilous fight,
O'er the ramparts we watched were so gallantly
    streaming?
And the rocket's red glare, the bombs bursting in air,
Gave proof through the night that our flag was still
    there.
Oh, say does that star-spangled banner yet wave
O'er the land of the free and the home of the brave?

That song reminds us of the persistent bravery that won and has sustained the freedom of our nation since the song's writing in 1814. This is why worship music is so powerful in our churches. It reminds us of the greatness and goodness of our God. It's really tough to lack hope when you are singing at the top of your lungs about the love and help of our God!

Prayers

In other places, we see prayers of praise telling all that God has done. These prayers are written down or memorized, to be repeated over and over as a reminder of the hope we have in him. To this day most Christians can recite the Lord's Prayer. But there are more prayers in Scripture that remind us of God's willingness to forgive, deliver, sustain, and strengthen us. Jesus himself prayed a great priestly prayer over us all in the gospel of John.

My prayer is not for them alone. I pray also for those who will believe in me through their message, that all of them may be one, Father, just as you are in me and I am in you. May they also be in us so that the world may believe that you have sent me. I have given them the glory that you gave me, that they may be one as we are one—I in them and you in me—so that they may be brought to complete unity. Then the world will know that you sent me and have loved them even as you have loved me.

—John 17:20–23

With these words, and others that I have not printed here, Jesus left us a promise that has encouraged the church since the first day he spoke this prayer. Here we can find the hope and the promise that God will not forget us or forsake us.

Stories

Every culture has hero stories. Christianity is no different. In fact, as Christians we have our own hero stories, *and* we get to share the hero stories from Jewish history. We have the story of Moses and the nation of Israel walking on dry ground through the Red Sea to show that God can overcome even impossible odds to save his people (see Ex. 14). We have the story of David and Goliath to remind us that God can defeat massive giants with young brave shepherds (see 1 Sam. 17). We have the story of Elijah and the prophets of Baal to show that one follower of God is greater than hundreds of followers of a lifeless idol (see 1 Kings 18). Then there are the stories of Jesus' life. Jesus calms a storm (see Matt. 8:23–27); Jesus heals ten lepers (see Luke 17:11–19); Jesus raises Lazarus from the dead (see John 11:38–44); and more. These stories remind us that Jesus has power over nature, sickness, and even death.

These reminders become even more important in times of darkness and fear. If these reminders are kept and repeated, they can guard us from despair. They can keep us from returning to the I-am of brokenness where this entire story began. In fact, that's where most of our stories began. Brokenness brought into our lives by sin left us hopeless and in despair.

But then God the Father "lavished" his love on us and called us "children of God" (1 John 3:1). Jesus the Son gave his life for us, "not wanting anyone to perish" (2 Pet. 3:9). God the Holy Spirit indwells us with fire so that we can be empowered to live our lives for him, through him, and see our world changed by him.

This is the great truth of Scripture: God loves us.

And if God truly loves me, then my I-am is set by him. I may actually not like who I am right now. Perhaps my I-am is broken or less than what it should be. But we know that God has dealt with people like us before. The stories tell us so. We know that God has delivered people from worse than our own situation before. The songs tell us so. We know that God loves us so much that he sent his only Son to die for us; Jesus loved us so much that he died on a cross and rose from the dead so that we could be forgiven. We know that God sent the Holy Spirit so that we could be changed from the inside out. The stories tell us so.

My I-am—my identity—no longer has to be all wrapped up in my failures and my past.

Through Christ, my identity is redeemed, bought back, set free, made whole.

No matter what I was, I am now a child of God!

Notes

1. Warren Farrell and John Gray, *The Boy Crisis: Why Our Boys Are Struggling and What We Can Do About It* (Dallas: BenBella Books, 2019), 46.

2. Farrell and Gray, *The Boy Crisis*, 46.

3. Kenneth Barker, ed., *NIV Study Bible* (Grand Rapids: Zondervan, 1985), 696.

4. John Wesley, *The Works of John Wesley: Complete and Unabridged*, 3rd ed., vol. 11, *Thoughts, Addresses, Prayers, Letters* (Grand Rapids: Baker Book House, 1984), 367.

5. David B. Guralink, ed., *Webster's New World Dictionary of the American Language* (New York: Prentice Hall Press, 1970), 43.

Books in
Coffee with the Pastor Series

- Mike Hilson, *King David* (Indianapolis, IN: Wesleyan Publishing House, 2019).
- Mike Hilson, *The Book of James* (Indianapolis, IN: Wesleyan Publishing House, 2019).
- Mike Hilson, *Nehemiah* (Indianapolis, IN: Wesleyan Publishing House, 2020).
- Mike Hilson, *The Book of Colossians* (Indianapolis, IN: Wesleyan Publishing House, coming in 2020).
- Mike Hilson, *The Books of 1–3 John* (Indianapolis, IN: Wesleyan Publishing House, coming soon).

Watch for these and other titles in the series at
www.wphstore.com.